FIRST FIGHTER

A History of America's First Team
1918 - 1983

by

Charles F. O'Connell, Jr.

June 1987

Office of TAC History
Headquarters Tactical Air Command
Langley Air Force Base, Virginia

Foreword

Tactical aviation has played a significant role in determining the outcome of man's conflicts ever since the first flimsy aircraft appeared over the battlefield. While the range, speed, and combat capabilities of tactical aircraft have improved, the basic functions of tactical airpower have not changed signficantly. Counter air, interdiction, close air support, reconnaissance -- missions familiar to early aviators -- remain the cornerstone of the tactical repertoire.

The 1st Tactical Fighter Wing occupies a unique place in the history of American tactical aviation. Its accomplishments in wartime, especially in World War I, are well known, as are the names of some of its most famous members of that era: Rickenbacker, Luke, Lufbery, and Campbell. Less well known, but no less signficant, is the unit's peacetime work. From its beginnings in France in May 1918 to the modern wing stationed here at Langley, the "First Team" has always been in the forefront in the development and testing of new fighter tactics, new operational doctrines, and new equipment. No other Air Force fighter unit can trace such a long history, and few can point with pride to a past full of such great accomplishments.

This mongraph traces the rich history of this distinguished unit. While the focus of the work is squarely on the unit itself, the narrative touches briefly on some of the broader issues that influenced the group's, and later the wing's, development. Because it does, this brief study also offers some insight into how tactical aviation developed into the potent force it is today.

ROBERT D. RUSS
General, USAF
Commander, Tactical Air Command

Preface

Most current and past members of the 1st Tactical Fighter Wing are aware that their unit has had a long and memorable history. Some of them might even be able to recount great moments in its history, probably drawing on their memories of stories of "Captain Eddie" Rickenbacker and Frank Luke. It is doubtful, however, that many of them have any real sense of just exactly how significant their wing's past has been.

First Fighter recounts a story that needed telling. A sense of the past can tie those of us privileged to serve in this unit today to the Rickenbackers, Lukes, LeMays, Maloneys, and countless others whose work and sacrifices in the past have helped to make the wing what it is today. We can all take great pride in our knowledge of where the wing has been, and if the past is any indication, we can look to the future with optimism and a strong sense of purpose. I heartily recommend this brief study to those who wish to know more of the history of this fine unit.

BUSTER G. GLOSSON
Colonel, USAF
Commander, 1st Tactical Fighter Wing

Introduction

This monograph grew out of discussions held in late 1982, when the leadership of the 1st Tactical Fighter Wing began to consider what it could do to celebrate the wing's upcoming 65th anniversary. The wing's commander, Brigadier General Eugene H. Fischer, vice commander, Colonel Robert K. Wagner, and executive officer, Lieutenant Colonel Ronald K. Shoemake, agreed to support my proposal to prepare an illustrated history of the wing.

A work intended to commemorate the wing's 65th anniversary finally appears, closer to the 70th anniversary than to the 65th. I was historian of the 1st Tactical Fighter Wing when I began work on this project in early 1983. In August of that year, I moved to the Tactical Air Command History Office. In December 1984, I became assistant chief of the TAC History Office. These events help to explain why this monograph appears under the imprimatur of the command and not the wing; they also, I hope, help to explain the delay in its completion.

Two commanders and two "bosses" supported my work. I completed all of the research and most of the writing during my time at the wing, when I served under General Fischer and later Colonel Henry Viccellio, Jr. At the TAC History Office, Mr Ben Goldman allowed me to complete the first draft of the text. His successor, Mr Robert J. Smith, "encouraged" me to finish the monograph. I hope the finished product justifies their support. My colleagues at the TAC History Office, including Dr Jim George, Dr Tom Crouch, and Dr John Smith, read and reread the manuscript. If factual errors or stylistic inconsistencies remain despite their best efforts, I bear full responsibility. John also prepared the index.

This monograph highlights, I think, the dangers inherent in losing sight of the past as a military organization develops. As the discussion of combat operations in World Wars I and II suggests, the failure to record, document, and (most importantly) learn from the tactical lessons of the First World War cost the group in the Second. A review of the unit's activities from 1946 to 1983 further suggests the important role history can play in shaping morale and esprit in good times and in bad. The organizational changes of the 1950's and 1960's were made with little thought given to the "First Team's" long history. No one could reasonably claim that the successes of the 1970's and 1980's grew directly out of the decision to reassemble the wing, but it seems to show, to this historian at least, that the wing's strong sense of its past contributed to the development of the dynamic spirit that provided the foundation for those accomplishments. I hope this brief study will contribute to the maintenance of that spirit.

CFO

Langley AFB, November 1986

TABLE OF CONTENTS

Preface	iii
Foreword	v
Introduction	vii
Table of Contents	ix
List of Photographs	xi
Chapter One, World War I	1
Chapter Two, The Inter-War Years	19
Chapter Three, World War II	43
Chapter Four, The Air Defense Era	59
Chapter Five, Back to TAC	73
Appendices	85
Appendix I, 1st Tactical Fighter Wing Lineage	87
Appendix II, Honors	89
II-1 Rickenbacker Congressional Medal of Honor	90
II-2 Luke Congressional Medal of Honor	91
II-3 Distinguished Unit Citation, 25 August 1943	92
II-4 Distinguished Unit Citation, 30 August 1943	93
II-5 Distinguished Unit Citation, 18 May 1944	94
II-6 Air Force Outstanding Unit Award, 1 March 1978	95
II-7 Air Force Outstanding Unit Award, 11 January 1985	96
Appendix III, Organization	97
III-1 5 May 1918 - 24 December 1918	98
III-2 1919 - 1934	100
III-3 1935 - 1941	102
III-4 World War II	104
III-5 3 July 1946	106
III-6 15 August 1947	108
III-7 1948 - 1949	110
III-8 31 December 1950	112

III-9	6 February 1952	114
III-10	18 October 1956	116
III-11	1 February 1961	118
III-12	16 January 1967	120
III-13	1 October 1970	122
III-14	1 July 1971	124
III-15	19 April 1976	126
III-16	15 June 1977	128
III-17	5 May 1983	130

Appendix IV, Group and Wing Commanders 133

Footnotes 135

    Chapter One 135
    Chapter Two 139
    Chapter Three 145
    Chapter Four 149
    Chapter Five 153

Index 155

List of Photographs

I-1	Major Bert M. Atkinson	14
I-2	Lieutenant Colonel Harold E. Hartney	15
I-3	Captain Edward V. Rickenbacker	16
I-4	Lieutenant Frank Luke, Jr.	16
I-5	The 94th Aero Squadron	17
I-6	Lieutenant A. F. Winslow	17
I-7	Major Raoul Lufbery	18
II-1	1st Pursuit Group Emblem	36
II-2	Curtiss P-6E	37
II-3	Boeing P-12E	37
II-4	Boeing P-26A	38
II-5	Consolidated PB-2A	38
II-6	Seversky P-35	39
II-7	Curtiss P-36C	39
II-8	Boeing P-12Es in Formation	40
II-9	Curtiss P-6E	41
II-10	Curtiss P-6Es in Formation	42
III-1	Lockheed P-38 Lightning	54
III-2	Lockheed P-38 Lightning	55
III-3	Lieutenant Herbert P. Hatch	56
III-4	Preflight Intelligence Briefing	57
III-5	Lockheed P-38s in Formation	58
IV-1	Lockheed P-80	68
IV-2	North American F-86D	69
IV-3	Convair F-102	70
IV-4	Convair F-106	71
IV-5	North American F-86s in Formation	72
IV-6	North American F-86D	72
V-1	McDonnell Douglas F-4	81
V-2	McDonnell Douglas F-15A	82
V-3	Flightline at Langley AFB	83
V-4	McDonnell Douglas TF-15A	84

CHAPTER ONE

World War I

On 15 January 1918, a small party of Americans arrived at the French village of Villeneuve-les-Vertus, located about ten miles south of Epernay. Ordered from Paris two days before, the little band, led by Major Bert M. Atkinson and composed of Captains Philip J. Roosevelt and John G. Rankin, six sergeants, and a civilian, formed the vanguard of the people and organizations that would, five months later, form the 1st Pursuit Group. Major Atkinson, fresh from meetings with Brigadier General Benjamin D. Foulois, Chief of the Air Service, American Expeditionary Forces (AEF), and Colonel William Mitchell, Air Commander, Zone of Advance, knew that the American people expected much from the Air Service. He also knew that the air arm could claim no real accomplishments to that point, even though America had been at war for more than nine months. Foulois and Mitchell therefore told Atkinson and his staff "to get started as quickly as possible."[1]

Major Atkinson wasted little time in organizing a staff for the "1st Pursuit Organization and Training Center" established at Villeneuve-les-Vertus on 16 January 1918. He appointed Captain Roosevelt adjutant and Captain Rankin supply officer, and they set to work. Despite their good intentions, the conditions Atkinson, Roosevelt, and Rankin encountered in France complicated their work. The American staff in Paris had assured them that Villeneuve-les-Vertus was a spacious, well-equipped airfield ready to receive the three pursuit squadrons then completing the training course at the advanced training school at Issoudun, where American pilots transitioned from the trainers they flew in the United States to the high performance fighters they would fly at the front. Combat-ready Spads supposedly sat at French factories, awaiting the arrival of the pilots from Issoudun to ferry them to the front. The Americans found, to their chagrin, that the staff in Paris had little grasp of the actual situation at the front.[2]

Villeneuve proved to be a first-rate airfield, but the French 12th Groupe de Combat occupied all its facilities. The squadrons training at Issoudun were far from being ready for combat at the front. As for the Spads, the French suggested that they might be able to supply some in six months or so, but French aviation officers reported that they had few they could spare at the time.[3]

Captain Rankin, the supply officer, sized up the situation. He used some of his funds to purchase a quantity of champagne, and with its help and a little innovative bargaining, he obtained shop space from the French unit at Villeneuve-les-Vertus. By the middle of February, about a month after their arrival, Major Atkinson and his growing Training Center staff had managed to build or borrow a barracks and hangar space for thirty-six aircraft. When Atkinson reported that these limited facilities were available, the American staff in Paris dispatched to the airdrome the squadrons that would soon make up the 1st Pursuit Group. The 95th Aero Squadron reported on 18 February 1918. The 94th Aero Squadron rolled into camp two weeks later, on 4 March. Neither squadron possessed any aircraft, but Major Atkinson and Captain James E. Miller, commander of the 95th, began pursuing some promising leads.[4]

The 94th and 95th Aero Squadrons had trained and travelled together since their organization on 20 August 1917, at Kelly Field, Texas. First Lieutenant J. Bayard H. Smith became the first commander of the 94th, while First Lieutenant Fred Natcher led the 95th.

When the two squadrons boarded a train at Kelly Field on 20 September 1917 for the trip to Mineola, New York, they consisted entirely of the enlisted echelon that would form the squadron's ground support element. Arriving at Mineola on 5 October, the squadrons reported directly to Aviation Mobilization Camp No. 2. Each unit completed training there in about three weeks and proceeded to Hoboken, New Jersey, where, on 27 October 1917, they boarded a ship for the trip to Europe. The two squadrons arrived at Liverpool on 10 November, spent about fourteen hours in a rest camp, boarded a steamer at Southampton, and sailed for France on 12 November. The 94th and 95th entered camp at LeHavre the next day, but their travels were not quite over. On 15 November the 95th moved to the Aviation Training Center at Issoudun. On 18 November the 94th moved to Paris, where it divided into seven detachments that immediately began advanced maintenance training in the region's airframe and aero-engine plants. The 94th reassembled in Paris and departed for Issoudon on 24 January 1918.[5]

After the 95th's personnel arrived at Issoudun in November, they received advanced training on the same types of aircraft they would operate at the front. The 95th thus found itself well along in its training when the 1st Pursuit Organization and Training Center announced its readiness to receive units in mid-February, and it became the first unit to be attached to the center. The 94th made good progress at Issoudun, however, and it reported to Villeneuve not long after the 95th. Captain Miller remained in command of the 95th when it arrived at Villeneuve; Major John F. Huffer commanded the 94th.[6]

The 1st Pursuit Center controlled a pair of combat units, but neither was ready for combat. The newly-assigned pilots and maintenance personnel were eager, but they had little with which to work. Major Atkinson had obtained only a handful of aircraft from the French, all Nieuport 28s, France's second-line fighter. The French reported that they had no surplus Spads available to equip the Americans, so Atkinson and his staff agreed that the units would see action sooner if the Americans accepted the more readily available Nieuport. On 26 February they received word that thirty-six Nieuports were waiting to be picked up at a factory near Paris. A contingent of pilots departed within hours, but bad weather delayed their return. The weather broke on 5 March, allowing fifteen pilots to take off for Villeneuve. Only six successfully completed the return flight that day. Weather and mechanical difficulties forced the others to land along the route. All the Nieuports reached Villeneuve by 8 March, and Atkinson assigned most of them to the 95th.[7]

Even as the 95th lay claim to the first sizable contingent of aircraft, the 94th made its bid for fame by launching, on 6 March 1918, the first patrol flown by an all-American squadron in France. At 0815, Major Raoul Lufbery led two young first lieutenants, Douglas Campbell and Edward V. Rickenbacker, on a two-hour patrol near Rheims. A German antiaircraft battery challenged the flight, but it encountered no aerial opposition, a fortunate circumstance, since neither Campbell's nor Rickenbacker's aircraft carried any armament. The two neophytes believed they had flown an uneventful patrol. To their surprise, the more experienced Lufbery calmly pointed out that he had spotted no less than ten Spads, four German fighters, and a German two-seat observation aircraft during the patrol. He also showed Rickenbacker holes in the fabric skin of the younger pilot's aircraft, a reminder of their brush with the German battery.[8]

I - World War I

The 95th made its first flights on 8 March 1918. These missions followed the pattern the 94th established during its first sorties. An experienced pilot, frequently either Major Lufbery or someone from the French group, led two or three Americans on a patrol over a quiet sector of the front. The Americans made great sport of these unarmed patrols, but the French expressed more concern. The initial patrols proved uneventful, but they were not without their risks. The frail Nieuports had several mechanical and structural faults, and engine trouble in a Nieuport contributed to the 1st Pursuit Center's first combat loss.[9]

Captain Miller, commander of the 95th, experienced engine trouble on a training flight on 8 March 1918. He landed safely at Coincy and returned to Villeneuve by truck. On 10 March he returned to Coincy to pick up his aircraft. On the way back to the Center, Miller stopped to visit some friends at the airfield at Coligny, where he borrowed a Spad and flew a patrol over Rheims in the company of two other pilots. German fighters attacked the flight; Miller died in the ensuing dogfight. Captain Seth Low assumed command of the 95th, but Major Davenport Johnson, who flew with Miller on his final flight, replaced Low on 15 March.[10]

As training operations continued and the pilots gained proficiency, morale in both squadrons soared. The Allies anticipated a German offensive on the Western Front, and the members of the two squadrons sensed that their real baptism of fire was at hand. With this prospect in mind, the members of the 94th began to discuss the design of a unit emblem. The 94th's commander, Major Huffer, suggested that the squadron use Uncle Sam's stovepipe hat. Lieutenant Paul Walters, squadron medical officer, suggested a variation on Huffer's theme. Recalling America's decision to enter World War I after a long period of neutrality, he proposed a device that would symbolize Uncle Sam throwing his hat into the ring. His squadron mates liked the idea, and one of the pilots, Lieutenant Paul Wentworth, volunteered to draw up some tentative sketches of the design. The result of Wentworth's work became one of the most widely-recognized unit insignias. The squadron's artists immediately began to apply the Hat-in-the-Ring emblem to the squadron's Nieuports.[11]

Even as they took brushes in hand, events occurred that brought the units of the 1st Pursuit Group Organization and Training Center into more active combat. The Germans launched a massive attack against the British lines to the north on 21 March 1918. The aircraft of the 94th and 95th still lacked guns, and the staff in Paris reported that the pilots were not proficient enough to face the Germans. Villeneuve was too close to the front to be occupied by partially-trained units, so the center moved to a quieter sector. Someone in headquarters also realized that most of the pilots had not received any formal air-to-air gunnery training. Consequently, on 24 March 1918, most of the pilots of the 95th were ordered to the gunnery training school at Cazaux, in southwestern France. On 31 March the headquarters of the 1st Pursuit Organization and Training Center moved from Villeneuve-les-Vertus to Epiez. The 94th, reinforced by the few pilots of the 95th who had already received gunnery training, flew to Epiez on 1 April.[12]

The center did not remain at Epiez for long. The field there was little more than a swamp. Aircraft regularly flipped over on landing, and the mud thrown back by flight leaders often broke the propellers of trailing planes during takeoffs. Because of pilot complaints and damage to the aircraft, the 94th left Epiez for Gencoult airfield near Toul. The 1st Pursuit

Center remained at Epiez, without squadrons. When the 94th transferred to Toul it was temporarily assigned to the French VIII Army as an "Independent Air Unit."[13]

The AEF air staff decided to transfer the 94th to Gencoult after determining that the squadron was ready to enter combat. Toul was an active sector, but the intensity of combat was low. The French used the region as a rest area for units rebuilding after an extended campaign and as a place to introduce newly-formed units into combat, and it seemed that the Germans used their side of the line for much the same purpose. Ground positions in the area were well-defined, with good communication links. French spotters at the front passed information about enemy aerial activity back to control centers and to the airfield, giving the 94th ample time to launch its aircraft.[14]

The squadron's first patrols from Gencoult followed a pattern similar to that it had established at Villeneuve-les-Vertus. Two or three Americans in unarmed Nieuport 28s, led by an experienced French pilot, flew patrols against enemy long-range photographic reconnaissance aircraft. The Air Service staff reported that:

> The fact that the American airplanes had no machine guns was due to the shortage of these guns that prevailed on the Western Front at the time, but the fact that the area in which they worked was so far back of the lines as to make the danger of enemy attack negligible, coupled with the fact that the morale effect of their presence was in all probability sufficient to insure the retreat of an isolated enemy photographic airplane, rendered this experience a valuable one.[15]

The 94th, still under the operational control of the VIII French Army, moved from Epiez to Gencoult on 10 April 1918. At about the same time, the squadron finally received a consignment of machine guns for its aircraft. Mechanics quickly installed and tested the guns, and the pilots of the squadron prepared themselves for the time they would actually be able to do something about the enemy aircraft they harassed during their training flights.[16] Two days later, the commander of the Army Air Service, French VIII Army, issued orders making the 94th responsible for control of the air over a sector of the front from St Mihiel to Pont-a-Mousson.[17] It seems unlikely that the pilots of the 94th knew of the AEF air staff's judgment that the enemy pursuit units facing it were "neither aggressive, numerous, nor equipped with the best type of machines."[18]

On Sunday 14 April, the pilots of the 94th stood alert as an active combat unit for the first time. Captain David Peterson led the squadron's first patrol with Lieutenants Reed Chambers and Eddie Rickenbacker. Lieutenants Douglas Campbell and Alan Winslow waited on alert at the airfield. Peterson led his flight north from Gencoult at about 0600, heading for Pont-a-Mousson. The weather was bad, and by the time they reached their patrol altitude of 16,000 feet Peterson had turned back for the field with engine trouble. Rickenbacker took over flight lead, and he and Chambers made four circuits of a twenty-mile stretch of front between Pont-a-Mousson and St Mihiel. By the time they turned for home a heavy blanket of fog had settled over the area. Rickenbacker entered the clouds and immediately lost sight of Chambers. Rickenbacker descended to about 100 feet before recognizing a landmark that enabled him to turn for Gencoult, where he landed safely. Chambers had not yet returned. At about 0800, as Peterson chided Rickenbacker for flying off in deteriorating weather, the

I - World War I

squadron operations officer received word that French spotters could hear German aircraft approaching the airfield. Campbell and Winslow took off immediately. Minutes after their departure a German Pfalz D-3 fell out of the clouds and crashed near the airfield. An Albatross D-5 followed it seconds later. The American pilots had no difficulty confirming these kills. Winslow received credit for the Pfalz, the 94th's first confirmed victory. Campbell was credited with the Albatross. The Americans landed about ten minutes after they scrambled. Both German pilots survived, and they reported that they had tried to intercept Rickenbacker's flight but became lost in the fog. Chambers eventually joined the festivities that followed.[19]

Bad weather settled in, so the 94th remained on the ground for several days, basking in the glow of its "opening day" successes. Captain James N. Hall and Lieutenant Rickenbacker shared a kill on 29 April, the squadron's only other victory that month. As the 94th gained combat experience at the front, the 1st Pursuit Operations and Training Center added additional squadrons behind the lines. The pilots of the 95th completed their gunnery training at Cazaux and returned to Epiez on 22 April. The 27th and the 147th Aero Squadrons reported to Major Atkinson's headquarters the same day. Both arrived without planes or pilots.[20]

The 27th Aero Squadron was organized as Company K, 3d Provisional Aero Squadron, at Kelly Field, Texas, on 8 May 1917, almost fourteen weeks before the 94th and 95th were organized. On 15 June, Company K was redesignated the 21st Provisional Aero Squadron. The Signal Corps then discovered that it had organized another 21st Provisional Aero Squadron in California on the same day, so on 23 June 1917 the unit at Kelly Field was redesignated the 27th Aero Squadron, with Major Michael Davis as its first commander. In mid-August the squadron left Texas for Toronto, Canada, for advanced training. After about a month in Canada the 27th returned to Camp Hicks, near Fort Worth, Texas. Major Harold E. Hartney, a Canadian native and Royal Flying Corps veteran who had the dubious distinction of being one of Baron Manfred von Richthofen's early victims, became squadron commander on 2 January 1918. The 27th received orders to move to New York on 11 January, but it did not leave Texas for Garden City, New York, until the 23d. When the squadron arrived, medical officers immediately placed it under quarantine for scarlet fever. During this interlude the Army transferred two officers and sixty enlisted men to other units. Medical authorities lifted the quarantine on 3 February, and the squadron moved onto a troop ship. Squadron personnel lived aboard the transport until 26 February, when it sailed for Liverpool. The 27th arrived in England on 5 March 1918, the same day the 95th received its first Nieuport 28s in Paris and the 94th reported to Major Atkinson at Villeneuve. On 23 March the 27th arrived at the Aviation Training Center at Issoudun.[21]

The 147th Aero Squadron arrived at Issoudun the next day. Organized on 11 November 1917 at Kelly Field under First Lieutenant John D. Morey, it completed its training and left New York for Liverpool on 5 March 1918. The squadron arrived on 18 March, proceeded to LeHavre on the 24th, and arrived at Issoudun late the same day. The 27th and the 147th trained together there for about a month. They reported to the 1st Pursuit Organization and Training Center on 22 April.[22]

The AEF transferred the 95th Aero Squadron from the training center at Epiez to the 94th's airfield at Gencoult on 4 May, the same day it directed the 1st Pursuit Organization and

Training Center to move from Villeneuve to Gencoult. As of that date the center controlled three squadrons, the 27th, the 95th, and the 147th. The 27th and 147th were training at Epiez. The 95th found itself strung out on the road between Epiez and Gencoult. The 94th, still serving as an independent air unit with the French VIII Army, flew daily patrols from Gencoult.[23]

The 1st Pursuit Group was organized at Gencoult, France, on 5 May 1918 under Major Bert M. Atkinson. Officers from the 1st Pursuit Organization and Training Center, which appears to have been dissolved at this point, filled most of the group staff positions. Headquarters, AEF assigned the 94th (relieved from its temporary assignment to the French VIII Army) and the 95th Aero Squadrons to the 1st Pursuit Group on the same day. The 1st Pursuit Group was, as its name suggests, the nation's first group-level fighter organization, but it was not the AEF's first flying group. That honor went to the 1st Corps Observation Group, organized in early April. The 27th and the 147th Aero Squadrons joined the group on 30 May.[24]

The group suffered a devastating loss two weeks later. On 19 May Major Raoul Lufbery, part of the group staff but flying with the 94th, took off to intercept a German intruder. He attacked the two-seater, but the German gunner hit Lufbery's Nieuport in the gas tank. The aircraft burst into flames. Lufbery rode the blazing machine down to about 3,000 feet, where he apparently jumped out of the aircraft. He wore no parachute; French villagers who witnessed his fall reported that he struck a fence, staggered briefly to his feet, then fell over dead. Lufbery had received credit for seventeen kills at the time of his death, although he may have scored at least that many more that were never confirmed.[25]

Lufbery's death stunned the group. He had helped to train many of the pilots, and they respected his courage and ability. The 94th and the 95th turned out in force for his funeral the next day. Lieutenant Kenneth P. Culbert of the 95th described the ceremony:

> As we marched to the grave, the sun was just sinking behind the mountain that rises so abruptly in front of Toul; the sky was a faultless blue and the air heavy with the scent of blossoms. An American and a French General led the procession, followed by a band which played the funeral march and "Nearer My God to Thee" so beautifully that I could hardly keep my eyes dry. There followed the officers of his squadron and my own, and after us, a group of Frenchmen, famous in the stories of this war, American officers of high rank, and two American companies of Infantry, separated by a French company. We passed before crowds of American nurses in their clean white uniforms and a throng of patients and French civilians. He was given a full military burial, with the salutes of the firing squad and the repetition of taps, one answering the other from the west .... Truly France and America had assembled to pay the last tribute to one of their bravest soldiers. My only prayer is that somehow, by some means, I may do as much for my country before I too go west - if in that direction I am to travel.[26]

Lieutenant Culbert died in battle - he "went west" - the next day.[27]

As the pilots of the 1st Pursuit Group helped lay Major Lufbery to rest, the members of

1 - World War I

the 27th Aero Squadron prepared themselves for their own initiation into combat. As part of this process, the pilots of the 27th met to consider a squadron insignia. They discussed several possibilities before Lieutenant Malcolm Gunn suggested a design he noticed in New York that struck his fancy. The Anheuser-Busch brewery used (and continues to use) an eagle for its corporate logo. Gunn suggested that the 27th adopt a variation of this design, an eagle with outspread wings and talons diving on its prey. A Corporal Blumberg drew a sample design on 18 May, and the other members of the squadron decided it would make an ideal insignia. The squadron continues to use a variation of this design, although a falcon replaced the eagle in 1924.[28]

The 27th (under Major Harold Hartney) and the 147th (under Major Geoffrey Bonnell) reported to Gencoult on 31 May. On the same day Lieutenant Douglas Campbell of the 94th became the nation's first "ace" when he shot down a German Rumpler observation plane over American lines near the village of Menil-la-Tours. The 94th took over the task of introducing the 27th to the intricacies of aerial combat, and pilots from the 94th led pilots of the 27th on their first patrols on 2 June. The 27th scored its first kill on 13 June, when four pilots combined to down an Albatross. By the end of June, as the 1st Pursuit Group prepared to move to a more active front, the group's four squadrons had accumulated twenty-seven confirmed kills, although pilots claimed to have shot down a total of fifty-eight enemy aircraft.[29]

Group headquarters warned its units to be prepared to move on short notice in early June, when allied intelligence advised that a German offensive was imminent. On 26 June the group dispatched an advance party from the 27th to set up shop at Tonquin airfield, a site about 150 miles west of Toul and some twenty-five miles southwest of Chateau-Thierry. The 1st Pursuit Group headquarters transferred to Tonquin on 29 June, the same day the group's fifty-four Nieuport 28s made the flight without incident. The group mustered all its organizations the next day, and the four squadrons each made patrols over the area to familiarize the pilots with the terrain. Combat operations began on 1 July.[30]

The move to Tonquin marked the end of the 1st Pursuit Group's formative period and the beginning of four months of almost continuous front line service. By about 1 July the group's four squadrons were competent, combat-ready organizations. Since April they had accounted for twenty-seven kills (seventeen credited to the 94th, six to the 95th, and four to the 27th) in the quiet Toul sector. The squadrons learned to fly and fight together, and the group staff gained valuable experience controlling operations. The move to the Marne front exposed the members of the 1st Pursuit Group to a more demanding combat environment.[31]

The United States had so little combat aviation experience that most of the 1st Pursuit Group's actions during this period established precedents. The move from Toul to Tonquin, for example, was one of the Air Service's first large-scale tactical relocations in the face of the enemy. The AEF air staff considered the move to be so successful and so carefully executed that the official history suggested that it "might almost be considered a model."[32]

Atkinson organized the group into three echelons. The first formed an advance party, dispatched by ground transportation, that "comprised sufficient personnel from each squadron to care for the arriving airplanes, to install the necessary telephonic liaison and to arrange for billeting the enlisted and commissioned personnel."[33] The flying squadrons comprised the second echelon, while the third consisted of the maintenance and support personnel who launched the aircraft and brought remaining equipment to the new operating location. Atkinson devised a simple and efficient mobility procedure that was deemed a noteworthy innovation at the time.[34]

The 1st Pursuit Group's operations on the Marne front marked the beginning of a period during which the Army Air Service began to develop operational and tactical procedures. When the group moved to the Marne front, it joined with the 1st Corps Observation Group and some French units to comprise the 1st Air Brigade, under Colonel Mitchell. Allied intelligence had detected a massive German buildup along the front and predicted a drive on Paris. To provide air cover for the upcoming offensive, the Germans deployed forty-six of their seventy-eight fighter squadrons, including Hermann Goering's Jagdeschwader I, the famed Richthofen Flying Circus. The quality and numbers of the opposition, along with the demanding requirements of the group's missions, forced the 1st Pursuit Group to adopt new tactics.[35]

Colonel Mitchell assigned the 1st Pursuit Group three missions. The four squadrons worked to allow American observation aircraft to operate freely, to prevent enemy observation aircraft from completing their missions, and "to cause such other casualties and inflict such other material damage on the enemy as may be possible."[36] The tactics adopted to protect American observation aircraft subsequently caused unnecessary losses, but the most immediate problem the group faced came from the numerically superior, aggressive, and experienced German squadrons. Lieutenant Harold Buckley of the 95th described the situation:

> ... the halcyon days were over. No longer could we hunt in pairs deep in the enemy lines, delighted if the patrol produced a single enemy plane to chase. Gone were the days when we could dive into the fray with only a glance at our rear. There was trouble ahead. The action we craved was at hand; we could sense it in the air like an approaching storm.... The sky around us was filled with Fokkers; instead of a lone two-seater or two, we counted the enemy in droves of twelve, eighteen, and twenty.[37]

The two-to-six plane formations of the Gencoult days gave way to squadron-strength patrols, twelve-to-sixteen plane formations divided into three flights. The lead flight attacked first, protected by the other two, which supported the first if the situation warranted. In practice, the flights frequently fought separate battles; the first attacked its target, usually enemy observation aircraft, while the other flights battled to keep escorting fighters off the backs of the lead section.[38]

Doctrinal difficulties compounded the tactical problems created by the need to fly and fight in large formations. The group fared well when it flew offensive patrols against German observation aircraft, but it suffered heavy casualties when it flew close escort missions in support of the 1st Corps Observation Group. While the escort missions proved to be great morale boosters to the crews of the observation aircraft, the pursuit pilots were less enthusiastic. The observation aircraft were slower than the fighters and they attracted clouds of German fighters. Directed to fly in a protective formation around perhaps one or two observation aircraft, the escorts yielded the initiative to the Germans. "Denied the possibility

I - World War I

of utilizing their maneuverability, speed or guns, they were easy prey."[39]

After suffering heavy observation and fighter losses, the American fliers adopted more successful tactics: the observation aircraft flew in larger formations, forcing attacking Germans to face the concentrated gunfire of their defensive armament. Escort support took the form of squadron-strength fighter sweeps flown ahead of and around the observation formations. This gave the fighters the initiative, since they could now attack as the Germans climbed toward the observation formation. Epic air battles involving several squadrons on each side sometimes developed.[40]

To further complicate the group's difficulties, a conversion from Nieuport 28s to Spad XIIIs began as the Marne campaign opened. The conversion took most of the month of July. The Nieuports were fragile aircraft, prone to shed fabric from their wings during violent maneuvers. Still, the 27th and the 147th preferred those "little fellows that responded more to the pilot's thought than to his touch" to what Major Hartney of the 27th called "those damned Spad machines."[41] The 94th and the 95th, on the other hand, had experienced more difficulty with Nieuports coming apart in mid-air and were delighted to get the Spads. The Spad was a sturdier and more powerful aircraft, but its Hispano-Suiza engine was more complex and more difficult to keep in tune than the Nieuport's Gnome rotary. The pilot transition and maintenance training process disrupted operations and effectively grounded each squadron in turn for several days, but the group flew what was available from day to day.[42]

The Chateau Thierry (or Aisne-Marne) campaign comprised two phases that lasted from 15 July to about 6 August 1918. The long-awaited German offensive formed phase one, from 15 July through the 18th. The Germans gained some ground, but the well-prepared Allied armies blunted the German drive. The Allies launched a counteroffensive that lasted from 18 July through early August. The 1st Pursuit Group saw continuous action throughout the campaign, with the 27th and the 95th performing especially well. Pilots frequently flew three or four two-hour sorties each day, often in the face of heavy opposition. The group flew observation escort, counter-observation and ground attack missions, with an occasional reconnaissance sortie added to the flying schedule. Losses were heavy: in July the group destroyed twenty-nine German aircraft, but lost twenty-three.[43]

Despite the difficulties encountered throughout the entire operation, the pilots of the 1st Pursuit Group "maintained their aggressive spirit, and attacked and fought successfully superior numbers of enemy planes."[44] The Air Service gave the group high marks for its operations:

> While it is true that several of our balloons were burned; that our ground troops were repeatedly harassed by machine gun fire; and that our corps air service suffered more severe losses than they anticipated, it is also true that the 1st Pursuit Group carried the fighting into enemy territory; that our corps air service, despite its losses, was always able to do its work, even the work of deep photography, and that enemy attempts at photography and visual reconnaissance were seriously interfered with.[45]

The group operated out of Tonquin and later Saints (occupied on 8 July) until about 20 August, supporting operations on the Chateau Thierry/Marne front and bringing its new

Spads into service. During the last ten days of August, the group witnessed a number of changes as it prepared for its next campaign. On 21 August Major Hartney, commander of the 27th Aero Squadron, replaced Major Atkinson as commander of the 1st Pursuit Group. First Lieutenant Alfred A. Grant replaced Major Hartney as commanding officer of the 27th. Major Atkinson assumed command of the 1st Pursuit Wing, 1st Army, AEF. The wing included the 2nd and 3rd Pursuit Groups and the Day Bombardment Group.[46]

Between about 22 August and 1 September, the group moved from Saints to Rembercourt, some twenty miles west of the town of St Mihiel on the Verdun/St Mihiel front. This move became part of the buildup for the American drive to eliminate the St Mihiel salient, and the group made the trip under the utmost secrecy. As the squadrons arrived at Rembercourt, they dispersed themselves around the field and camouflaged their aircraft and other equipment. The group kept its deployment hidden while it attempted to mask the American buildup along its front from German observation aircraft.[47]

The attack began on 12 September; American forces eliminated the German positions in about four days. During the campaign the 1st Pursuit Group covered the front from Chatillion-sous-les-Cotes to St Mihiel, flying observation escort and anti-observation sorties. Extremely bad weather during the first three days of the offensive forced American aircraft to low levels, where they attacked German observation balloons and harassed troops on the ground. The attack caught the Germans in the midst of evacuating the salient, and American aircraft took a heavy toll of the retreating enemy. The weather improved on the 14th, but German air opposition centered on the southern flank of the salient covered by the 1st Pursuit Wing. As a result, the 1st Pursuit Group concentrated on ground attack throughout the campaign. Although ground operations ended on the 16th, air operations continued for another week to ten days.[48]

As at Chateau Thierry, combat filled the 1st Pursuit Group's days. The pilots again flew many sorties each day, frequently landing only to take on more fuel and ammunition. The pace of action took its toll on both planes and pilots; as the ground campaign drew to a close, Hartney ordered the group to reduce its operations to give mechanics time to make permanent repairs on the Spads, many of which were beginning to look like flying sieves from ground fire. The pilots were as worn out as the aircraft: on 16 September, Lieutenant John Jeffers of the 94th fell asleep while returning from a patrol. His Spad continued its flight on course, losing altitude slowly. Jeffers woke up in time to level out and crash on a hill not far from the airfield. He escaped injury.[49]

Another short lull followed, as the American army redeployed for the Meuse-Argonne offensive. The 1st Pursuit Group rested and received replacements for the aircraft and pilots lost during the campaign. One noteworthy change of command occurred during this interval: on 25 September, Lieutenant Rickenbacker replaced Major Kenneth Marr as commanding officer of the 94th Aero Squadron.[50]

Rickenbacker took command of a squadron "which seemingly had never lived up to its early promise."[51] When he checked on the status of the squadron's kills, he found that the "presumptuous young 27th had suddenly taken a spurt, thanks to their brilliant Luke, and now led the Hat-in-the-Ring Squadron by six victories!" Rickenbacker immediately convened

I - World War I

his pilots and announced that "no other American squadron at the front would ever again be permitted to approach our margin of supremacy." Within a week, the 94th had overtaken the 27th and never relinquished the lead.[52]

After his talk with the pilots, Rickenbacker next approached the squadron's mechanics who, he reported, "felt the disgrace of being second more keenly than did we pilots."[53] Not surprisingly, Rickenbacker later noted that from that time on the squadron's aircraft were always in top mechanical condition.[54]

Lieutenant Rickenbacker resolved to lead by example. A squadron commander had administrative responsibilities, but they interested him less than the real matter at hand. He passed these duties to subordinates.

> To avoid the red-tape business at the aerodrome - the making out of reports, ordering materials and seeing that they came in on time, looking after details of the mess, the hangars and the comfort of the enlisted men - all this work must be placed under competent men, if I expect to stay in the air and lead patrols. Accordingly I gave this important matter my attention early next morning. And the success of my appointments was such that from that day on I never spent more than thirty minutes a day upon the ground business connected with 94's operation.[55]

At about this time - late September 1918 - the 1st Pursuit Group reached its operational peak. All four squadrons were experienced, and staff officers at all levels had served through at least two major campaigns. As of the end of September, after about six months of combat, the group was credited with one hundred kills, achieved at a cost of fifty-seven casualties.[56] Major Hartney, the group commander, "found in the other squadrons the same ultra-fine quality of officers and men of which I had been so proud in the 27th, courageous, well-trained, decent, loyal and intelligent."[57] During the last seven weeks of the war the 1st Pursuit Group scored an additional 102 kills at a cost of fifteen of its pilots.[58]

The United States Army launched its final offensive of the war on 26 September, when the American First Army began the Meuse-Argonne offensive. The terrain favored the defenders, and the Germans had organized a formidable defensive system. By this time the AEF staff had come to appreciate "the morale effect of aviation,"

> ... and it was felt that the necessity of supremacy of the air was needed more by American arms in these operations than perhaps ever before, to produce the greatest results. It needed the morale supremacy, so easily enhanced by a predominance of ground troops, of low-flying airplanes to carry Americans over the awful terrain of the Meuse under trying weather conditions.[59]

The 1st Army air staff assigned the 1st Pursuit Group the task of providing that low-level support during the offensive. The staff ordered the group to clear the front of enemy observation balloons and low-flying aircraft. The 1st Pursuit Wing, especially the 2nd and 3rd Pursuit Groups, provided top-cover for the 1st Pursuit Group. It also provided escort for American bombers and observation aircraft.[60] The staff knew that the decision to commit roughly one-third of the fighter force to tactical air support might jeopardize air superiority, but they believed that it was "more important that enemy aviation, including balloons and airplanes, low and full in sight of the advancing troops, should be destroyed at all costs."[61]

Committed to low-altitude defense suppression and air support operations, the 1st Pursuit Group reverted to the small formations and stalking tactics that characterized its earlier service on the Toul front. The group flew most of its missions during the last seven weeks of the war at low altitude, attacking enemy observation aircraft and heavily-defended observation balloons, although pilots showed no reluctance to take on enemy fighters that slipped past the group's top cover.

Perhaps no one was any better at this dangerous work than Lieutenant Frank Luke of the 27th. Luke specialized in attacking enemy balloons, a risky process since the balloons floated on tethers at known altitudes and enjoyed the protection of aircraft and mobile flak batteries. Luke attacked these balloons fearlessly. His only close friend in the 27th, Lieutenant Joseph Wehner, often flew top cover while Luke went after a balloon. Neither attracted any particular attention until the start of the Meuse-Argonne campaign, when their work against the German balloons brought them both fame and death.[62]

On 18 September, Luke and Wehner were attacking a balloon line when Wehner noticed seven Fokkers stalking Luke's Spad. Wehner threw himself at the Germans, disrupting their attack and alerting Luke. The odds were too great, however, and Wehner was killed. Luke tore into the Germans, and in about ten minutes destroyed three balloons and two of the Fokkers. Luke was never noted for his caution, but he showed a tendency to take even greater risks after Wehner's death. Hartney grounded him for a time, but to no avail.[63]

On Sunday, 29 September, Luke took off alone to take on enemy balloons along the front. At 1905 he destroyed one near Dun-sur-Meuse. Another fell shortly thereafter at Buiere Farm. He then shot down two pursuing Fokkers before claiming a third balloon near Milly at 1912. Badly wounded and flying a damaged plane, Luke strafed a German unit he found in Murvaux. He then made a forced landing near the town. He drew his pistol and fired on the German troops sent to capture him. Luke died in the ensuing gun battle. He was later awarded the Congressional Medal of Honor for his actions on this mission.[64]

The 1st Pursuit Group continued to fly low-level missions until the end of the war. On 7 October, the 185th Night Pursuit Squadron, led by Lieutenant Seth Low, was assigned to the Group. The 185th was organized at Kelly Field on 11 November 1917 and trained as a night fighter unit after arriving in France. Its prey were the giant German bombers that made nightly forays into Allied territory, and its tactics were simple: after receiving word that the Germans were in the vicinity, a pilot took off, climbed for altitude, and shut off his engine to listen for the intruders. When a pilot felt he was too low he restarted his engine, climbed, cut the engine again, and resumed his aural search. The squadron achieved no confirmed kills during the month it was at the front, but Major Hartney may have shot down a German bomber using this method.[65]

The 1st Pursuit Group achieved remarkable success during the last six weeks of the war. In October the group's five squadrons destroyed fifty-six of the enemy at a cost of thirteen American planes. The 94th set the pace with twenty-eight kills. November was an even more

I - World War I

remarkable month. During the first ten days of the month the four day-squadrons destroyed forty-five enemy aircraft or balloons without a loss. The 94th, which claimed America's first World War I kill, also received credit for the last aerial victory, a Fokker destroyed by Major Maxwell Kirby on 10 November. The Armistice took effect the next day.[66]

The 1st Pursuit Group ended the war with 202 confirmed kills. Rickenbacker was America's "Ace-of-Aces" with twenty-six kills, twenty-two aircraft and four balloons. Luke scored eighteen kills, four aircraft and fourteen balloons, while Lufbery received credit for seventeen kills, all aircraft. By squadron, the 94th received credit for sixty-seven and a half kills; the 27th, fifty-six; the 95th, forty-seven and a half; and the 147th, thirty-one. The squadrons achieved these totals at a cost of seventy-two American casualties, killed, wounded or captured. The 27th lost twenty-two; the 95th, nineteen; the 94th, eighteen; the 147th, ten; and the 185th, three. The four day-squadrons of the 1st Pursuit Group accounted for approximately 38 percent of the Army Air Service's 526 confirmed victories in World War I.[67]

On 17 November orders from the American staff in Paris relieved the 94th Aero Squadron from its assignment to the 1st Pursuit Group, assigned it to the 5th Pursuit Group, Third Army, and directed it to prepare to accompany elements of the American Army across the Rhine. The squadron departed Rembercourt on 25 November and occupied the former German airfield at Moors four days later. On 7 December advanced parties of the group's remaining squadrons departed Rembercourt for Colombey-les-Belles, where the 1st Pursuit Group disbanded on 24 December 1918. The 95th returned to the United States on 1 March 1919 and demobilized at Garden City, New York, on 18 March. The 27th and the 147th arrived at Hoboken the next day. The 27th ended the war as it began it, in quarantine in New York, this time with the 147th. The two squadrons demobilized in April. The 94th ended its service with the Third Army on 9 April 1919 and arrived at Hoboken on 31 May. It demobilized at New York on 1 June. Even as the World War I squadrons completed their demobilization, however, the War Department began organizing a new 1st Pursuit Group at Selfridge Field, Michigan.[68]

Photo I-1

Major Bert M. Atkinson,
first commander of the 1st Pursuit Group
(5 May 1918 - 21 August 1918)

Photo I-2

Lieutenant Colonel Harold E. Hartney, commander of the 27th Aero Squadron and second commander of the 1st Pursuit Group

Photo I-3

Captain Edward V. Rickenbacker
94th Aero Squadron

Photo I-4

2nd Lieutenant Frank Luke, Jr.
27th Aero Squadron

I - World War I 17

Photo I-5

The 94th Aero Squadron

From left to right, front row: Lt L. Prinz; Lt H. H. Tittman; Lt F. Ordway; Lt W. W. Smith. Middle row: Lt W. G. Loomis; Lt C. A. Snow; Lt M. E. Green; Lt A. F. Winslow; Capt K. Marr; Lt E. V. Rickenbacker; Lt J. A. Meissner; Lt T. C. Taylor; Lt G. W. Zacharias. Back row: Lt H. Coolidge; Lt A L. Cunningham; Lt W. W. Chalmers; Lt J. H. Eastman; Lt A. B. Sherry; Lt J. Wentworth; Lt R. Z. Cates; Lt E. Clark; Lt J. N. Jeffers.

Photo I-6

The 94th Aero Squadron

Lt A. F. Winslow with 14 April 1918 Kill,
a Ptalz D-3

Photo I-7

Maj Raoul Lufbery
The 94th Aero Squadron

CHAPTER TWO

The Inter-War Years

The War Department created a new 1st Pursuit Group between late April and mid-August 1919, when it dispatched two-man cadres of the 27th, 94th, 95th, and 147th Aero Squadrons to Selfridge Field, Michigan. New recruits and veterans from other flying units arrived to assume their places in the squadrons, and by late summer the process was complete. The Army activated the 1st Pursuit Group on 22 August 1919. The unit then took its place as one of the three group-level organizations that constituted the Army's air arm for most of the next decade. Like the 3rd Attack and the 2d Bombardment Groups, the 1st Pursuit spent most of the next twenty-two years testing aircraft and tactics developed to exploit the potential of the aerial weapon.[1]

The group's initial tour in Michigan lasted less than ten days. On 28 August the four squadrons departed by train for Kelly Field, Texas. The newly organized group headquarters, under the command of Captain Arthur E. Brooks, left Selfridge for Kelly two days later. For the next three years the group remained in Texas, where it operated the Advanced Pursuit Training School.[2]

The leaders of the Army Air Service knew that the organizational and operational lessons learned during World War I would shape postwar activities, but in the haste to demobilize after the war the Army broke up units without giving adequate thought to its future needs. As the organizational situation stabilized at the end of the summer of 1919, the army began to devise better considered defense plans, and it also recognized that the proper application of the lessons of the war required a carefully planned training program. The decision to use the 1st Pursuit Group as an "Advanced Pursuit Training School" reflected this thinking.[3]

The Army used the pursuit school to build an effective fighter force in stages, beginning with the fundamentals of flying and culminating in group-strength fighter maneuvers. The course of instruction for pilots at Kelly consisted of a twenty-week program of classroom and in-flight training. Topics covered included squadron, group, and air service history, the history of aircraft and aero-engine design, development, and maintenance, aeronautical theory, military and aerial strategy and tactics, weather, navigation, operational procedures, and organizational theory and practices. Pilots received hands-on experience in aircraft and engine maintenance. They also flew a 72-hour program that covered formation flying, aerobatics, air-to-air and air-to-ground gunnery, reconnaissance and patrol tactics, and emergency procedures. In addition, pilots served liaison tours with bombardment and attack units and with infantry, cavalry, armor, and artillery formations to improve intraservice understanding and coordination. Pilots also made a number of tethered and free lighter-than-air flights.[4]

After completing this part of the syllabus, the pilots joined a squadron, where their training entered another stage. They spent somewhat less time in the classroom, more in the air. When the pilots learned to fly and fight as part of a larger unit, training progressed to the group level. This phase of the course included some group-strength formation flights and squadron-versus-squadron air combat, but the pilots again returned to the classroom for work in the fundamentals of officership, command, management, and staff activities. While the Advanced Pursuit Training School trained the pilots, the group's mechanics and support personnel kept busy with their own course of classroom and field work. They practiced their trade by working on aircraft used to support the flight training syllabus.[5]

The 1st Pursuit Group's work at the Advanced Pursuit Training School, initially at Kelly and later at Ellington Field, Texas, established a solid foundation that the group built on during the next decade. During the 1920s the group was the Army Air Corps' only group-level pursuit organization. As such, the Army repeatedly called on it to evaluate new aircraft designs, test equipment under a variety of operating conditions, demonstrate aircraft and unit capabilities, and practice advanced tactics during Air Corps and Army maneuvers. The group also flew numerous public relations flights throughout the eastern and mid-western United States. The years in Texas forged the group into a competent, cohesive unit. The group used this training as the basis for more demanding projects undertaken during the Twenties.

The 1st Pursuit Group prepared to return to Michigan in late June 1922. It still consisted of four squadrons, although the 147th had been redesignated the 17th Aero Squadron on 3 March 1921. The air echelon, consisting of the 17th, 27th, 94th and 95th squadrons and led by the group's commander, Major Carl Spatz (later Spaatz) departed Ellington Field on 24 June 1922. The ground component followed on 27 and 28 June. The long aerial deployment was a novelty, and the public and the press followed the group's progress closely. The aircraft arrived at Selfridge Field on 1 July 1922.[6]

Selfridge served as the group's home for many years. The field was situated on a 641-acre site located northeast of the city of Mount Clemens, a suburb of Detroit. It was named after Lieutenant Thomas E. Selfridge, one of the Army's first pilots, who died in the crash of a Wright Flyer flown by Orville Wright on 17 September 1908. The site was reclaimed swampland, and poor drainage plagued the field for years. Nonetheless, the group settled into its new home and began preparations for an event that became a hallmark of the 1st Pursuit.[7] The National Air Races took place at Selfridge Field from 7-14 October 1922. Included in the program was the first running of the Mitchell Trophy Race. Brigadier General William Mitchell donated the John L. Mitchell Trophy to the Air Service in memory of his brother, lost in action during World War I while serving with the 1st Pursuit Group. Mitchell aimed to stimulate the development of better pursuit aircraft, and the races, held from 1922-1930 and from 1934-1936, became a key proving ground for new pursuit designs. The first Mitchell Trophy Race seems to have been open to all qualified entrants, but the entry criteria soon became more restrictive. To be eligible for the Mitchell Race, a pilot had to be a Regular Army officer and a member of the 1st Pursuit Group who had served at Selfridge for at least one year and had accumulated at least 1,000 total flying hours. A final qualification made the race especially significant for the group's pilots: a pilot could fly in only one Mitchell Trophy Race. Lieutenant Donald F. Stace of the 27th won the first Mitchell race. He made four circuits of the twenty-mile course in his Thomas-Morse MB-3 at an average speed of 148.1 mph.[8]

The Mitchell Trophy Race provided a moment of excitement each year, but most of the group's regular operational activities throughout the decade were far less glamorous. As the Air Corps' only pursuit group, the War Department took special pains to ensure that the 1st maintained a high state of readiness. It conducted quarterly inspections and mobilization tests

II - The Inter-War Years

during 1923, 1924, and 1925. The units performed well during these tests, but to maintain its edge the group itself conducted its own regular inspections and practice alerts. These types of activities have long dominated the peacetime operating schedule of all types of military organizations; the interwar 1st Pursuit Group was no exception.[9]

In 1924 the War Department sanctioned unit emblems. On 21 January 1924, the Adjutant General approved the emblem of the 1st Pursuit Group. The design of the device reflected the unit's history. The colors of the shield, green and black, represented the original Army Air Service. The five stripes stood for the group's five original squadrons, and the five crosses symbolized the group's five major World War I campaigns: Champagne-Marne, Aisne-Marne, St Mihiel, Verdun, and Meuse-Argonne. The colors of the crest, with its golden winged arrow on a sky-blue disc, were the colors of the Army Air Corps. The crest bore the group's motto: "Aut Vincere Aut Mori" - "Conquer or Die." Revisions made in 1957 deleted the crest and added the scroll at the base of the shield.[10]

The Adjutant General also approved unit emblems for the squadrons. The "Great Snow Owl," white on a black background, became the official emblem of the 17th Pursuit Squadron on 4 March 1924. The next day the World War I-vintage "Kicking Mule" emblem was officially assigned to the 95th Pursuit. On the same day, 4 March, the 27th's "Diving Eagle" became a "Diving Falcon," because the War Department did not want to appear to be endorsing a brand of beer.[11]

Commercial considerations forced the War Department to change the emblem of the 94th. During the early 1920s Eddie Rickenbacker decided to produce a line of automobiles that bore his name. Rickenbacker adopted, as the company's logo, the hat-in-the-ring device the 94th had used as a unit emblem during the war. Again in an effort to avoid appearances that it was promoting a product, the Adjutant General's office decided, on 6 September 1924, that the 94th would use the Indian-head device formerly used by the 103rd Aero Squadron, a World War I unit formed when the members of the Lafayette Escadrille transferred to the Army Air Service after the United States entered the war. Even though the Rickenbacker was not a commercial success and the company soon went out of business, the 94th continued to use the Indian-head insignia until 1942.[12]

The group also opened a satellite facility in 1924. On 18 May thirty enlisted men left Selfridge for Oscoda, Michigan, to establish an "Aerial Gunnery Camp" for the 1st Pursuit Group. Facilities at the camp were spartan at first, but during the course of the next decade the group made numerous improvements at the site. Such improvements were necessary, because the squadrons of the 1st Pursuit returned to Oscoda regularly for gunnery practice against towed and ground targets. These deployments usually included one of at least squadron strength during January or February, intended to test aircraft in severe winter conditions, and a larger deployment during the spring devoted to gunnery practice. The group also regularly rotated squadrons through Oscoda to prepare them for special tests or maneuvers.[13]

Beginning in about 1925, the group participated in exercises, demonstrations, and maneuvers, events the War Department used as combined training and public relations exercises. Public and congressional interest in aviation was high. The group flew fast, nimble, pursuit planes that attracted the attention of earth-bound taxpayers wherever they appeared.

At the same time, the War Department wanted to test evolving doctrines and tactics that would enable the air arm, especially tactical aviation, to work effectively with other branches. As a result, the group's Selfridge training schedule often aimed to prepare the unit for demanding summer and fall activities.

The 1925 training cycle was typical. Between May and October the group completed four formal tactical inspections and participated in a mobilization test on 4 July that saw it dispatch planes to Alpena, Oscoda, and Frankfort, Michigan, Washington, DC, and Youngstown, Ohio. On 26 February, group commander Major Thomas G. Lanphier led a flight of twelve PW-8 aircraft from Selfridge to Miami, Florida, in an attempt to set a dawn-to-dusk flight record. The flight reached Macon, Georgia, by mid-afternoon, when bad weather forced the planes to the ground. The aircraft finally reached Miami on 2 March. The War Department made use of the contingent's presence on the East Coast to put on a demonstration for Congress and the press.[14]

The demonstration was held at Langley Field, Virginia, on 6 March. A static display on the flightline enabled the assembled congressmen to examine the planes. The aerial portion of the demonstration, which occupied most of the afternoon, used as its scenario a simulated attack on a battleship silhouette. The 1st Pursuit's twelve aircraft opened the attack by strafing the silhouette and dropping light bombs. The fighters then laid a smoke screen to cover the attack of heavy bombers and attack aircraft, which the fighters protected and attacked in turn.[15]

The spectators seemed duly impressed with this demonstration, but some contact with members of Congress brought the group rather less favorable attention. On 26 March 1925 Lieutenant Russell Minty's aircraft failed to clear a stand of trees and crashed shortly after takeoff from an airfield near Uniontown, Pennsylvania. The pilot escaped injury but his passenger, a Pennsylvania congressman, was not so lucky. He was badly cut and bruised and suffered a broken collarbone and several broken ribs. The congressman's reaction to this mishap is not recorded, but the group diary noted Minty's transfer to non-flying duties on 27 March.[16]

The unfortunate Lieutenant Minty had a bad year in 1925. Returned to flying status, he joined five other 1st Pursuit Group pilots detailed to fly from San Francisco to New York to test a new transcontinental air-mail route. The group left Selfridge on 15 July. On 31 July Minty escaped injury when his P-1 crashed and sank in the Des Moines River during a night flight from Cheyenne, Wyoming, to Chicago. The circumstances of the lieutenant's mishap served as an unfortunate precursor of the group's later involvement with carrying air mail.[17]

An inspection conducted by Major General Mason M. Patrick, Chief of the Air Service, on 29 January 1926 ushered in another busy year for the 1st Pursuit Group. After winter maneuvers at Oscoda, the group deployed a detachment of eighteen aircraft (eight PW-8s, seven P-1s, two P-1As, and one C-1) to Wilbur Wright Field, Dayton, Ohio, on 19 April to participate in Army Air Service maneuvers. The purpose of this exercise was "to train the Air Brigade Staff and the lesser Staffs in the technique of air force units during concentration of ground forces up to a point just before the actual meeting of the ground forces." It was the second of three such exercises: the first, in 1925, simulated an attack on the coast and focused

II - The Inter-War Years

on the staff work required to concentrate aircraft at the point of attack; the 1927 exercise simulated air operations during the land battle. The 1926 maneuvers began with a command post exercise. The flying units based subsequent tactical operations on situations that had developed during the first phase.[18]

In addition to the 1st Pursuit's seventeen aircraft, the Army Air Service detachment at the maneuvers included thirteen aircraft from the 2d Bombardment Group and twelve planes from the 3d Attack Group. Two aircraft formed a "Provisional Observation Group." The main tactical problems covered during the operations phase included pursuit patrols versus bomber and attack aircraft, with special emphasis on the development of pursuit tactics against both types. The group also worked on offensive tactics, including rendezvous, attack formations, and escort tactics. During seven days of flying the 1st Pursuit Group flew 154 sorties and 186 hours. In his report on the maneuvers, Brigadier General James E. Fechet, Air Service Chief of Staff, expressed concern that pursuit tactics, which he feared were becoming too inflexible, exposed the pursuit planes to defensive fire for too long. The maneuvers also pointed out that the units needed more practice in long-range formation flying.[19]

The maneuvers detachment returned to Selfridge on 1 May 1926. Later that month, the group sent three P-1s, three pilots, and twenty mechanics to Camp Anthony Wayne, Pennsylvania, where they served as part of the Air Corps (the Air Service became the Air Corps on 2 July 1926) Demonstration Detachment at the Declaration of Independence Sesquicentennial Exhibition at Philadelphia. The other members of the group continued to carry on training at Oscoda and Selfridge throughout the summer. On 26 September six pilots flew their P-1s to Kelly Field, Texas, for temporary duty in support of the filming of the movie Wings.[20]

The group's activities peaked in 1927 and 1928. Increasing interest in the effects of cold weather on operations took twelve aircraft to Canada from 24-30 January 1927. The army wanted to "determine the limitations of aircraft and equipment when operating under deployed conditions in a severe climate" and to test various types of skis for use on aircraft. The Canadian government welcomed the test contingent as a good-will gesture, and the War Department approved the flight on 23 January. The group deployed thirteen aircraft (six P-1As, four P-1Bs, two P-1s, and one Douglas C-1 transport), thirteen pilots and six mechanics from Selfridge to Ottawa the next day.[21]

Conditions in Canada proved ideal for the test. The aircraft arrived in the midst of a blinding snowstorm, and "the poor visibility and the difficulty of keeping the landing area clear of pedestrians somewhat hindered the Flight in landing." The landing area on the Ottawa River was covered with twenty inches of snow, and the aircraft's rear skids broke through the crust, causing damage to each of the aircraft. Canadian mechanics helped install large disks on the tail skid to support the aircraft.[22]

Temperatures got no lower than 20° F during the night of 24-25 January, but this was enough to chill the engines thoroughly. Mechanics filled them with hot oil the next morning, but they were still too cold to start. "Hot bricks placed in the air intakes close to the carburetor, used to vaporize the ether priming" did not work well either. The mechanics finally borrowed a fire hydrant defroster from the Ottawa Fire Department, forced steam into the engines, and got them started. The detachment commander noted with interest, however, that the P-1Bs equipped with self-starters turned over much more readily on the cold morning.[23]

The Canadian flight's luck with the weather continued. The aircraft departed Ottawa in the early afternoon of 25 January. They ran into another blinding snowstorm, landed on the Ottawa River, took off when the storm cleared, landed when another squall developed, then took off a third time. The 100-mile flight took about two hours, and the section finally arrived at Montreal. Mechanics drained the water and oil from the engines, but that still left the pursuits poorly prepared for the -20° F they faced the night of 25-26 January. Three-man crews, working ninety minutes on each aircraft, got all planes started the next morning.[24]

Flying on the 26th was uneventful, but the thermometer dropped to -22° F that evening. The crews delayed the takeoff of their flight to Buffalo, New York, because "it was doubtful whether it would have been possible for the pilots to have withstood the cold for four hours in their present type of flying equipment."[25] By about 1300 eleven of the twelve pursuits were ready to depart, but a sticking carburetor prevented the twelfth from starting. Nine aircraft took off about 1400, but a storm forced them down near Fisher's Landing, New York. The aircraft "taxied to a position in the shelter of the boat house and wharves on the shore of the little cove." The storm did not abate, so the pilots stayed in Fisher's Landing overnight. The nine-plane flight reached Buffalo on 29 January.[26]

In the meantime, the three aircraft left behind in Montreal took off at about 1530 on 28 January, but poor visibility forced them to turn back. They took off again at about 1100 the next day and reached Alexandria Bay, New York, before a radiator leak in one plane forced the flight down. The three took off and reached Woodville, New York, when one aircraft's broken oil line forced them down again. Two continued while the pilot of the damaged aircraft repaired the oil line. The two-plane flight landed near Irondequoit Bay when a radiator overheated. On takeoff the plane that suffered the radiator leak lost its engine. The three planes finally staggered into Selfridge between 30 January and 1 February. The nine planes from Buffalo arrived at Selfridge on 30 January.[27]

The flight commander's recommendations came as no shock to those who followed the flight's progress. The Air Corps needed aircraft with engine block heaters and self-starters, a stronger tail skid for its aircraft, and a warmer and more comfortable winter flying suit.[28]

The 1927 maneuver/demonstration cycle began on 27 April, when Captain Hugh M. Elmendorf, commander of the 94th, led a five-plane flight from Selfridge to Bolling Field, DC. The flight then proceeded to Edgewood Arsenal, Maryland, where mechanics added smoke generators and the pilots learned how to lay the smoke in conjunction with armor and infantry attacks. This flight then made its way to Pope Field, North Carolina; Atlanta, Georgia; Fort Benning, Georgia (where it put on tactical demonstrations for the instructors and class at the Infantry School); Mansfield, Louisiana; Galveston, Texas; and finally Kelly Field, Texas, where the Army held its 1927 maneuvers.[29]

A second demonstration flight of eight P-1s, led by Captain Frank H. Pritchard, left Selfridge on 3 May. This group flew demonstration flights at Fort Riley, Kansas, and Fort Sill, Oklahoma, before arriving at Kelly Field on 10 May. The next day the group launched

II - The Inter-War Years

eighteen more P-1s for Kelly, this detachment led by Major Thomas G. Lanphier, the group commander. The detachment left Selfridge at 0630. It arrived at Kelly at 1815 after making two intermediate stops, where waiting group mechanics serviced the aircraft. When the maneuvers began on 15 May, the 1st Pursuit Group had thirty-one P-1s deployed at Kelly Field, with thirty-one pilots, twenty-one mechanics, and twelve support specialists.[30]

During seven days of maneuvers (15-21 May), the group flew ground attack, bomber attack, bomber escort, air superiority, and defensive missions. In addition, the group participated in a day-long series of demonstration flights for visiting dignitaries on 21 May. Umpires noted that "the operations of the First Pursuit Group as a whole during these maneuvers were very good,"[31] but in his critique Brigadier General James E. Fechet, the air commander at the maneuvers, warned that "conditions for air operations here were almost ideal and would not necessarily be obtained in actual operations. In other words, the airplanes here were operated under conditions which were better than we could expect in warfare."[32] Under these conditions the group flew 236 operational and 23 demonstration sorties and approximately 400 hours.[33]

The group returned to Selfridge on 25 May and had barely settled in when it undertook another large-scale demonstration flight. On 12 June the group flew twenty-two P-1s nonstop from Selfridge to Bolling Field to act as an escort for Colonel Charles A. Lindbergh on a tour through several east coast and midwestern cities. Stops on the Lindbergh tour included New York, St Louis, Selfridge, Ottawa, and Buffalo. During each of these visits the aircraft of the 1st Pursuit Group provided demonstration flights and static displays. The escort detachment returned to Selfridge on 8 July, but the group had not seen the last of Colonel Lindbergh. On 4 November 1927, he reported to Selfridge for fourteen days of active duty training with the group. His training included a trip to the Oscoda range.[34]

Not long after the Lindbergh escort flight returned to Selfridge, the 1st Pursuit Group bid goodbye to one of its original units. On 31 July 1927 the War Department inactivated the 95th Pursuit Squadron and transferred it to March Field, California, where it was activated on 1 June 1928 and attached to the 7th Bombardment Group. The squadron soon traded its pursuits for attack aircraft, and in World War II the squadron, now designated the 95th Bombardment Squadron, flew its B-26s in the Mediterranean theater of operations, where the P-38s of the 1st Fighter Group often escorted them to their targets.[35]

The hectic pace of the group's activities continued during 1928. Training continued to occupy most of the group's time. There were no maneuvers in 1928. Instead, the group deployed twenty-two P-1s, five C-1s, twenty-six officers and thirty enlisted men under Major Lanphier, group commander, on a twenty-four day demonstration tour to the Army's service schools. This group left Selfridge on 29 April and proceeded to Bolling Field, where it added four pursuits previously sent to the Edgewood Arsenal. Those aircraft participated in an Air Corps demonstration at Bolling on 29 April and then flew to Langley Field for a series of tactical demonstrations. The Langley program included static displays, mock combat between pursuits, bombers, and attack planes, aerobatics, ground attacks, and an aerial review.[36]

From 5-22 May, a thirty-four plane (twenty-six P-1s, eight C-1s) detachment from the 1st Pursuit Group visited the Army's major posts and schools. The tour took the group from

Langley to Fort Bragg; Fort Benning (Infantry School); Maxwell Field (Air Corps Tactical School); Fort Sill (Artillery School);Fort Riley (Cavalry School); and Fort Leavenworth (Command and General Staff School). Each stop featured a similar program: static displays, acrobatics, aerial reviews, and tactical demonstrations with the service arm the school specialized in. Eight of the P-1s returned to Selfridge on 22 May, but eighteen flew to Des Moines, Iowa, for more demonstration flights. This detachment returned to Selfridge on 26 May. During the tour the group flew 765 sorties and more than 1,430 hours.[37]

While the Des Moines flight involved an unusually large contingent of aircraft, it typified another activity the 1st Pursuit Group participated in repeatedly throughout the 1920s. Many communities, large and small, built municipal airfields during the decade. These airfields often opened with an air show, and the Air Corps, aware of the opportunity for publicity these shows offered, responded readily to local requests for an Air Corps display at the opening. Since the pursuits had long since proved they could get into and out of even the roughest landing field, the 1st Pursuit Group frequently sent small detachments to airport openings. During the summer of 1928, these missions took group aircraft to many sites throughout the midwest.[38]

The group's training followed established patterns through the last year of the decade. The largest deployment of 1929 saw the group send fifty pursuits to central Ohio for maneuvers in May. While operations at the maneuvers were conducted without major incident, a critique of the performance of the pursuit aircraft noted that "it is quite obvious our training methods and our tactics as applied to pursuit, are not now satisfactory."[39] The report repeated some of the criticism levelled at pursuit tactics during World War I: pursuit units placed too much emphasis on tight formations, too little on effective attack tactics. As a result, only the lead plane in a formation delivered aimed fire. The rest fired on his cue, spraying a cone of bullets in the general direction of the target. These tactics forced wingmen to spend too much time watching the leader, too little watching for enemy aircraft.[40] Other activities during 1929 followed similar patterns: inspections, demonstration flights, equipment tests, Oscoda deployments, and airport openings.[41]

Overall, the Twenties were a productive decade for the 1st Pursuit Group. It responded well to the challenge of being the Air Corps' only group-level pursuit organization, and developed a reputation as a dynamic, well-trained force, prepared to respond skillfully to the operational demands the War Department placed on it. The group maintained a high degree of organizational stability. It even enjoyed the benefits of using tried and tested, if somewhat dated, equipment. While the unit flew a mix of obsolescent World War I aircraft during its stay in Texas, by 1924 it had converted to the Curtiss PW-8/P-1 series it used for the remainder of the decade.[42]

The 1930s produced a different set of challenges. During that decade, the group introduced at least six new aircraft types into the Air Corps inventory. It also provided cadres for newly formed squadrons and groups. But even as it carried on these activities, the pace of its regular training activities continued unabated.

The 1st Pursuit Group began the decade with a cold weather test flight that forced a detachment to operate in the face of extremely difficult conditions. On 7 January 1930 the

II - The Inter-War Years

group's mechanics positioned eighteen P-1s, two C-9s, a C-1 and an 02-K observation aircraft on the ice of Lake St Clair, adjacent to Selfridge Field, in preparation for the takeoff of the 1930 "Artic Patrol Flight." The primary purpose of the flight was to "test the efficiency of planes, personnel, and equipment under the most severe winter conditions." A secondary object of the flight was to "obtain first-hand experience on the value of shortwave radio in connection with Army Air Corps operations in remote sections and covering long distances." To this end, one of the cargo planes carried a complete radio set. The flight would proceed from Selfridge to Spokane, Washington, and back via stops in Minnesota, Wisconsin, and North Dakota.[43]

The flight was scheduled to take off on 8 January, but a sleet storm made even the iced-over lake too slippery for operations. The sleet storm also ushered in a warming trend, however, and during the evening of 8 January sentries noted that the radio aircraft seemed ready to break through the ice. All hands turned out to drag it to dry land. The group waited for better weather, and by the morning of 10 January the temperature had dropped enough to permit safe operations. The pursuits departed Selfridge at 0905 and arrived at Duluth, Minnesota, via St Ignace, Michigan, at 1520. The transports followed, arriving at Duluth by 1620. The observation aircraft, carrying H. J. Adamson, a representative of the Assistant Secretary of War for Air, developed engine trouble and stayed at Selfridge.[44]

The group proceeded to Minot, North Dakota, on 11 January. That night, the temperature plunged to -20° F. After a starter ripped a frozen engine apart, the crews decided to wait for the transports to bring engine heaters. The transports arrived that afternoon, but one broke an axle on landing. On the morning of the 13th the pursuits took off for Great Falls, Montana. Leaking radiators caused delays, and the flight began to get strung out along the route. By nightfall on 13 January, the main body had reached Great Falls. One landed at Hosey, Montana, with a broken piston, and three spent the night at Havre after darkness prevented them from reaching Great Falls.[45]

In the face of sub-zero temperatures and a howling blizzard, three pursuits and a transport reached Spokane on 17 January. Thirteen more arrived at about 1600 on 19 January. As his pilots, numbed with cold and exhausted, trickled in, the 1st Pursuit Group Commander, Major Ralph Royce, telegraphed Washington that "having battled forces of King Winter ten days and won from them secrets of how they intend to aid enemies of United States in wartime, the First Pursuit . . . stands defiantly on the ice of Newman Lake, 15 miles east of Spokane . . . and rests . . . while battle wounds are healed." As of this point the detachment had lost only one pilot, hospitalized at Great Falls with an infected foot.[46]

The aircraft took off for home on 23 January. The first leg took the crews from Spokane to Miles City, Montana, via Helena. The flight departed Miles City on schedule the next day, but poor visibility forced the aircraft to land on a farm owned by A. H. Arnold. The group lost an aircraft when one pilot crashed less than 100 yards from the Arnold home. It nearly lost a second when Major Royce plowed through three wire fences during his landing. The first six planes of the flight reached Bismarck on 25 January, with the rest arriving the next day. At the close of flying on the 26th, fifteen pursuits had reached Fargo. When the pursuits landed at Minneapolis the next day, Major Royce could at least account for all the planes with which he had left Selfridge. The radio plane was disabled in Minneapolis, but the other two transports were on hand and ready to continue the flight. The observation plane, late leaving Selfridge, followed the pursuits for a few days, then returned to Dayton. Seventeen pursuits stood at Minneapolis; Arnold kept watch on the wreckage of the eighteenth outside his front door. The pilot with the infected foot rejoined his comrades at Minneapolis; all personnel, less the observation crew, were on hand as well.[47]

The eighteen fighters and two transports flew to Wausau, Wisconsin, on 28 January. The next day the pursuits flew from Wausau to Selfridge via Escanaba, Michigan, ending the Arctic Patrol Flight of 1930. The flight demonstrated that the Army had largely ignored the recommendations made after the Canadian flight in 1927. The pilots complained that their flight suits remained excessively bulky and not warm enough. The Air Corps provided electric engine heaters, but the mechanics preferred to light "plumber's pots" under the aircraft to keep them warm. The little pots served the group well during the flight. The open fire blazing a few feet below the engine did not harm the aircraft.[47]

The group stayed close to home after the return of the Arctic Patrol Flight. Training continued as the group prepared for the next maneuvers, scheduled for April at Mather Field, California. The group sent the equivalent of about two squadrons to the West Coast. Three groups of six pilots each departed Selfridge by rail in early to mid-March on the way to Seattle, Washington, where they picked up the group's first consignment of Boeing P-12Bs. These eighteen aircraft proceeded to Mather after the pilots completed their pre-acceptance checks. Group maintenance personnel began to deploy to Mather on 23 March 1930. The group launched twenty-two P-1s and two C-9s daily from 25 March through 27 March, but bad weather forced the flight to return to Selfridge each day. The P-1s, led by Major Royce, finally took to the air on 28 March and reached Mather via Chanute Field; Fort Crook, Nebraska; Cheyenne, Wyoming; Reno, Nevada; and Salt Lake City, Utah, on 2 April. The maneuvers lasted for about three weeks. On 28 April the group left Mather for Salt Lake City, Denver, and Cheyenne. A flight of eighteen P-12Bs and nineteen P-1s (the deployment cost the group three aircraft and one pilot) returned to Selfridge on 2 May 1930.[48]

Eight days later, on 10 May, the group dispatched twenty-one P-1s to Aberdeen Proving Ground, Maryland, to serve as defensive forces in a joint Air Corps/Anti-Aircraft Service exercise. This force returned to Selfridge on 19 May, just in time to bid farewell to nineteen P-1s of the 94th Pursuit Squadron that left on 23 May to participate in Joint Army-Navy exercises in the New York City area. They returned to Selfridge on 30 May.[49]

The group devoted the summer of 1930 to the usual round of tactical training, demonstration flights, and airport dedications, but it soon faced a new challenge. On 2 October the Army activated the 36th Pursuit Squadron at Selfridge Field. The new squadron, destined to form part of the 8th Pursuit Group, was attached to the 1st Pursuit and staffed with a cadre drawn from each of the group's three squadrons and the group headquarters. The 36th eventually drew seven officers and 101 enlisted personnel from the 1st Pursuit. The 36th remained at Selfridge, attached to the 1st Pursuit Group, until mid-June 1932, when the Air Corps transferred the squadron to Langley Field.[50] The War Department continued to use the 1st Pursuit Group as a depot of sorts: on 1 December it directed the group to send sixteen of its new P-12s to Mather for use by the 20th Pursuit Group.[51]

II - The Inter-War Years

Patterson Field, Ohio, hosted the 1931 maneuvers, and again the 1st Pursuit sent a large contingent. The 36th Pursuit Squadron, still attached to the group, apparently used its training time well: on 1 May 1931 the four squadrons held a "fly off" to determine which would serve as the group's demonstration unit during the maneuvers. The 36th won this competition handily.[52] The group deployed 85 pursuits and seven transports to Dayton on 15 May. After approximately three weeks of performing what were by now fairly standard maneuver operations - patrol, ground attack, and bomber escort and attack - the group returned to Selfridge on 7 June.[53]

The onset of the Great Depression gave the 1st Pursuit several additional responsibilities. In 1931, the group participated in several air shows staged to benefit the unemployed. Group involvement ranged from two- and four-ship flights to squadron strength deployments to, for example, Indianapolis on 27 September 1931 and New York City on 16 October of the same year. Beginning in 1933, the group saw a handful of its officers detailed to work with the Civilian Conservation Corps, a New Deal program designed to put unemployed youth to work on various conservation projects.[54]

The most significant of the 1932 deployments saw a group strength movement of sixty-six aircraft (twenty-three P-6Es from the 17th; twenty-two P-12Es from the 27th; and twenty-one Y1P-16s from the 94th) to Chicago on 12 June for the George Washington Bicentennial Military Tournament. On the same day, the 1st Pursuit Group again became a three-squadron organization when the 36th Pursuit Squadron moved to Langley and the 8th Pursuit Group.[55]

The group's yearly operational schedule included more than just a deployment or an occasional airshow. As during the Twenties, the more noteworthy events were part of a training program that still included periodic deployments to Oscoda, daily training flights in the Selfridge area, and occasional trips to various schools and arsenals to test new equipment or tactics. Airport openings still drew at least a small detachment. Equipment changes came more rapidly. As the list of aircraft deployed to Chicago in June 1932 showed, the group had discarded its P-1s in favor of a number of more advanced designs.[56]

The P-6Es flown by the 17th were improved versions of the Curtiss Hawk line. Powered by a 600 hp Curtiss V-1570C engine, the Hawk had a top speed of 197 mph, a service ceiling of about 25,000 feet, and a range of 572 miles with its normal 100 gallon fuel load. The 27th flew Boeing P-12Cs, Ds, and Es. This design featured an all metal fuselage and a 600 hp Pratt & Whitney radial engine. The P-12 was somewhat slower than the P-6, with a top speed of 189 mph, but it had a higher service ceiling (26,300 feet). The range of the two types was similar: the P-12E's was 580 miles.[57]

In 1932 the 94th Pursuit Squadron flew Berliner-Joyce Y1P-16s (later P-16s). While the P-16 was roughly the same size as the P-6s and P-12s, it carried a two-man crew, a pilot and a rear gunner. Equipped with a Curtiss V-157A engine, the P-16 had a top speed of 175 mph, a service ceiling of about 25,000 feet, and a range of 650 miles. The Army Air Corps procured only twenty-five of these planes, and it apparently assigned all of them to the 94th.[58]

The pace of the group's training activities accelerated during 1933. On 6 January the Air Corps organized a Provisional Cold Weather Test Group at Selfridge, composed of five pursuits (P-6E, P-12C, D, E, and Y1P-16, all from the 1st Pursuit) and two B-6As from the Langley-based 20th Bombardment Squadron. The group proceeded to Sault Sainte Marie, Michigan, for tests and a tactical exercise with the 2d Infantry on 14 February, then moved to Duluth for more tests on the 23d. The tests completed, the Provisional Cold Weather Test Group disbanded on 15 March 1933.[59]

The 1933 maneuver cycle consisted of an Air Corps anti-aircraft exercise in southern Ohio and Kentucky. The group began deploying maintenance and staff personnel on 20 April, and by the time the exercise began on 15 May the 1st Pursuit had fifty-nine aircraft available for service in the maneuver area. The 94th was based at Patterson Field, Ohio, and attached to the 3d Attack Group; the 17th and 27th were based at Bowman Field, Kentucky, and used by the defense. For the exercise, an infantry detachment, a signal unit, and the 325th Observation Squadron, Organized Reserve, augmented the group.[60]

The 1933 exercise tested the antiaircraft net. The Bowman Field detachment spent most of the period from 15-24 May on alert, responding to aerial incursions tracked by a ground net and plotted by the group staff. The exercise also tested the applicability of radio to air defense. Some of the defending fighters carried radios, so the net spotted and tracked intruders and helped position interceptors for attacks. Bad weather grounded the pursuits for several days. When this happened, the group staff practiced tracking attack formations. From the air defense standpoint, the maneuvers were quite successful. During the final phase of the exercise the group completed eighteen of nineteen daylight interceptions, while the only night intercept attempted failed. The group returned to Selfridge on 25 May.[61]

The 1933 World's Fair at Chicago kept the group busy throughout the summer. On 1 July a 72-plane formation led by the 1st Pursuit Group's commander, Major George H. Brett, performed an aerial demonstration in conjunction with the opening of the fair. On 15 July the group launched a 42-plane formation under the new group commander (as of 11 July), Lieutenant Colonel Frank M. Andrews, to escort the Italian Trans-Atlantic Flight of twenty-one Savoia-Marchetti S-55s under General Italo Balbo from Toledo to Chicago. On 18 July, the group again put seventy-two planes in the air for a demonstration over Chicago in honor of the Italians. The next day the group again launched seventy-two aircraft to participate in a farewell display for the Italians. The flight then escorted the Italian bombers eastward to Toledo before returning to base.[62]

The 1st Pursuit Group had sixty-nine planes in service on 1 January 1934. These included one P-6A, one XP-6C, and sixteen Y1P-16s assigned to the 94th, and eleven miscellaneous cargo, observation, and training aircraft.[63] The year began with a scheduled series of winter deployments to Oscoda, but on 9 February the group received a message from Major General Benjamin D. Foulois, Chief of the Air Corps, advising it to be prepared to assign planes and pilots to air mail duty. Two days later President Franklin D. Roosevelt ordered the Air Corps to carry the mail while the administration resolved contract problems with commercial carriers.[64]

War Department directives called for the 1st Pursuit Group to provide sixteen planes and thirty-five pilots for air mail duty, although the group eventually assigned about fifty pilots, including Lieutenant Curtis E. LeMay of the 27th. Air Corps pilots in general were ill-

II - The Inter-War Years

equipped for the tasks they faced, and their equipment was not up to the test. The pilots had little training in night flying, the aircraft lacked adequate instruments, and ground facilities for cross-country flights were lacking. Bad weather compounded the problems. The result was a disaster. From 11 February to 23 June 1934, when the last officer from the group returned from air mail duty, group pilots were involved in ten crashes or forced landings that cost the Air Corps a similar number of aircraft. The group suffered two fatalities. On 22 February Lieutenant Durward O. Lowry of the 94th became the first of twelve Air Corps pilots to die carrying the mail when his parachute became tangled in the tail surfaces of an O-39 he was forced to abandon near Toledo, Ohio. The group's other fatality occurred on 26 April when Private First Class Donald Gagnier died in a motorcycle accident while performing air mail courier duty.[65]

On 22 February, the same day Lieutenant Lowry died, another group pilot escaped with serious injuries when he flew his P-12E into the side of a mountain near Uniontown, Pennsylvania. The next day group pilots were involved in two crashes and two forced landings. All four aircraft, two O-39s, a P-6E, and a Y1P-16 were destroyed, but the only injury was a broken leg suffered when a pilot landed on a barn roof in Freemont, Ohio, after abandoning his aircraft. Lieutenant Newton Crumley, 27th, and Private First Class William G. LeTarte, 17th, probably suffered the greatest indignity on 2 April, when they were forced to jump from a burning B-6A near Winfield, Pennsylvania. Both landed safely, but they received cuts and bruises, and Private LeTarte suffered a broken leg, when the civilian "Good Samaritan" who picked them up after they landed lost control of his automobile and crashed down a mountainside while taking them to town.[66]

The group bid an undoubtedly fond farewell to the air-mail duty in June and resumed a more normal training schedule. It spent most of the rest of 1934 rotating crews through Oscoda, while the 17th Pursuit began converting to Boeing P-26As, a low-wing, all-metal monoplane, fitted initially with a 550 hp Pratt and Whitney R-1340-27 Wasp engine. The aircraft had a top speed of about 235 mph, a service ceiling of 27,400 feet, and a range of 745 miles.[67] Lieutenant LeMay ended a five-year tour with the 27th on 22 September 1934, when he was reassigned to the Hawaiian Department. On 10 October Lieutenant Colonel Andrews relinquished command of the group to Major Ralph Royce.[68]

On 20 January 1935 another "Provisional Cold Weather Test Group" formed at Selfridge. By 1 February, when the group left Selfridge, it consisted of a collection of aircraft that included just about every model in the Air Corps' front-line inventory. The 1st Pursuit contributed three P-26As, three YP-12Ks, and the detachment commander, Major Ralph Royce. Three O-43As from the 12th Observation Group were also assigned. A C-27A joined on 23 January, followed by two B-12As from the 7th Bombardment Group on 25 January. The 3d Attack Group contributed three A-12s, the last aircraft added before the group began its month-long cold-weather flight test.[69]

Leaving Selfridge on 1 February, the group proceeded to its first stop, Alpena, Michigan, where it remained overnight. The group's itinerary over the next four weeks took it to Newberry and Hancock, Michigan; Duluth, Minnesota; Grand Forks and Minot, North Dakota; Great Falls, Helena, Miles City, and Billings, Montana; Bismarck, North Dakota; St Paul, Minnesota; Wausau, Wisconsin; and finally back to Selfridge Field on 27 February. The

Air Corps officially disbanded the test group on 5 March. While several aircraft sustained varying degrees of damage due to rough landings and equipment failures, the test group suffered only one serious accident. On 7 February Lieutenant Daniel C. Doubleday of the 27th was severely injured when his P-26A spun in and was demolished on Portage Lake, Hancock, Michigan. The test group encountered the full range of winter weather conditions: a blizzard in northern Michigan, a thaw at Duluth, and dust storms and fog in Montana.[70]

On 1 March 1935 the War Department established General Headquarters Air Force (GHQAF) at Langley Field, Virginia, "to command and control the Air Corps tactical organization."[71] The headquarters, under Major General Frank M. Andrews, former 1st Pursuit Group commander, controlled three GHQAF Wings; on 1 March the 1st Pursuit Group was assigned to 2d Wing, GHQAF. On the same date the 38th Pursuit Squadron, attached to the 1st since its organization on 1 August 1933, was inactived, redesignated a long range amphibian observation squadron, and assigned to the 3d Wing, GHQAF. The 56th Service Squadron was activated and, with the 57th Service Squadron, assigned to 2d Wing, GHQAF and attached to the 1st Pursuit Group. The 17th, 27th, and 94th Pursuit Squadrons had their enlisted components slashed by two-thirds, from 132 to 43. Much of the rest of the month of March was spent reassigning personnel and adjusting to the new command structure.[72] Between 17-19 May the group deployed to a camp established near Flint, Michigan, for a field test of the new GHQAF organization. A further mobility test was conducted from 5-10 June, when the 57th Service Squadron and the 27th Pursuit deployed on short notice to Kent County Airport, Grand Rapids, Michigan. The group completed both deployments without incident.[73]

The pace of training accelerated in 1936. During February, the 17th and the 27th passed through the gunnery range at Barksdale Field, Louisiana. From 20 May through 5 June, the group conducted field exercises at its Oscoda range. The summer training cycle culminated in August, when the 27th deployed twenty-three PB-2As and the 94th twenty-eight P-26As to Chanute Field, Illinois, for Second Army maneuvers. This contingent deployed on 1 August. While en route, the flight intercepted bomber and attack formations moving to Illinois from Langley and Barksdale. The group returned to Selfridge the next day and operated from its home base for the remainder of the maneuvers, except for brief deployments to Bowman Field and Fort Knox, Kentucky, on 6-7 August. Two full-strength squadrons, one each from the 2d Bombardment and the 3d Attack Groups, also operated from Selfridge for the maneuvers, which lasted until 20 August.[74]

Group support functions were reorganized on 1 September 1936. On that date the Group Headquarters and the 56th and 57th Service Squadrons were inactivated, consolidated, and redesignated Headquarters and Headquarters Squadron, 1st Pursuit Group. At the same time the Station Complement, Selfridge Field, was redesignated Air Base Headquarters and Third Air Base Squadron.[75]

A number of service organizations supported the 1st Pursuit Group since its activation in 1918. During World War I, Air Parks 1, 2, and 4 provided support. In late June 1921, Air Park No. 2 was redesignated the 57th Service Squadron and assigned to the 1st Pursuit Group. The 57th served with the 1st at Selfridge throughout the Twenties and Thirties, providing a maintenance and support echelon above the squadron level. Personnel transferred regularly

II - The Inter-War Years

between the 57th and the group's tactical components, and pilots assigned to the 57th flew the group's transports, which were also assigned to the service squadron. Each of the pursuit squadrons had, in addition to its complement of pilots, a maintenance component that consisted of a crew chief for each aircraft plus a number of specialists, including weapons specialists, airframe mechanics, and as the aircraft grew more complex, instrument and radio technicians. The 57th provided major maintenance support, including periodic overhauls and major structural repairs. The 57th also had sections devoted to supply, transportation, security and personnel.[76]

The group hosted the twelfth running of the Mitchell Trophy race at Selfridge Field on 17 October 1936, the last of seventeen events conducted that day at the base to benefit Army Relief and the Mount Clemens Community Fund. The 1st Pursuit and several visiting formations kept the crowd, estimated at 40,000 people, entertained with a variety of aerial displays and races, including competitions for the Mount Clemens, Boeing, and Junior Birdmen trophies, the latter presented to the air reserve officer who won the "Junior Birdmen Speed Dash." Lieutenant John M. Sterling won the Mitchell Trophy for completing the five-lap, one hundred-mile race at an average speed of 217.546 mph.[77]

The Air Corps organized yet another winter test detachment, this one called the "Cold Weather Equipment Test Group," at Selfridge in late January 1937. The 1st Pursuit contribution to the test group consisted of the 27th Pursuit Squadron, which flew to Oscoda on February 2d "to participate in intensive cold weather equipment tests."[78] A week later, on 9 February, the 27th returned to Selfridge but continued to participate in cold-weather tactical problems until 24 February, when the Air Corps disbanded the test group.[79]

The 1st Pursuit Group brought a new generation of fighter aircraft into the inventory in 1937, when it took possession of its first P-35 and P-36 aircraft. Lieutenant Colonel Royce flew the first P-36 from the Curtiss plant at Buffalo, New York, to Selfridge on 7 April. While the group was still equipped with the metal and fabric, fixed-landing gear, open-cockpit Boeing P-26, the new designs featured retractable landing gear, all metal construction, and enclosed cockpits. The P-26's 600 hp engine gave it a top speed of about 235 mph. Powered by a 1,050 hp Twin Wasp, the P-35A had a top speed of about 305 mph. The Curtiss P-36 Hawk, powered by the same engine as the P-35, was capable of 313 mph at 10,000 feet. The P-36 Lieutenant Colonel Royce delivered was a test model, designated Y1P-36. Following tests in May 1937 the Air Corps awarded Curtiss a contract for 210 Hawks - the largest Army fighter order since World War I.[80] The new designs, which "displayed an aesthetic elegance as they flashed through the sky," served the group as a bridge between the P-26 and the aircraft it would fly in World War II.[81]

Although the group was converting to more modern aircraft, it still took its P-26 and PB-2s to Muroc Dry Lake, California, for the 1937 Air Corps maneuvers. On 1 May sixteen transports, carrying a 168-man advance party, left Selfridge. This party arrived at Muroc the next day as the 27th, with fifteen PB-2As, and the 94th, with twenty-eight P-26Cs, left for California. On 3 May the 55th Pursuit Squadron, twenty-eight P-26As from Barksdale, arrived and was attached to the 1st Pursuit. More aircraft arrived at Muroc on 4 May, when the 27th was brought to full strength with the attachment of eighteen PB-2As from the 8th Pursuit Group. (The squadron's full strength was twenty-eight aircraft; five of the aircraft that flew out with the 27th belonged to the headquarters detachment.) Transports brought additional enlisted detachments from Selfridge on 6 and 10 May. At 0800 on 10 May the full-strength 1st Pursuit Group - 27th and 94th assigned, 55th attached - went on alert as the maneuvers began.[82]

This exercise pitted the group's fighters against bombers and attack aircraft in antiaircraft tests, a scenario much like the one used in 1933 in southern Ohio. The group staff plotted intruders and vectored on-station pursuits to intercept them. Operations on 11 May were typical. At 0300 the group command post learned of bombers approaching the patrol area. The 27th scrambled at 0313; the 55th followed at 0322; the 94th remained in reserve. A formation of eighteen attack planes entered the air defense zone at 0327. The 27th attacked the intruders at 0341 and 0351. The 94th scrambled at 0400, just before the attackers gassed the airfield at Muroc with real tear gas and simulated mustard gas. Elements of the 27th intercepted a bomber formation at 0427. Another formation from the same squadron met the bombers at 0437, while a third group faced still more attackers at 0447. The 27th picked up yet another attacking group over Muroc at 0459. The fighters landed at dispersed airfields at 0525. The three squadrons scrambled again at 1430, and the 55th made its first interception five minutes later. The 55th picked up more attackers at 1440, 1455, 1515, and 1522. The 27th made its attacks at 1450, 1504, and again at 1518. The group landed at 1550. The next day's battle began at 0320. The group maintained this schedule for twelve days, through 21 May, although the schedule usually called for only one sortie per day. A tired 1st Pursuit Group returned to Selfridge on 26 May.[83]

The group followed a similar schedule for the rest of the decade. In 1939 its P-36s, especially those of the 27th, sported experimental camouflage schemes that included such bizarre combinations as green, yellow, orange and white; lavender, "bottle green," olive drab, orange and white; forest green, lavender, orange and white; and gray, lavender, olive drab, and forest green.[84]

On 23 October 1940 the 17th Pursuit Squadron was relieved from assignment to the 1st Pursuit Group and transferred to the Philippine Department. Leaving Selfridge on 31 October, the squadron served in the defense of the Philippines until the spring of 1942 when the remnants of the squadron, fighting as infantry, were destroyed at Bataan. The War Department carried the squadron as an active unit, but it was not operational from the fall of the Philippines until 2 April 1946, when it was deactivated.[85]

The group was short a squadron, but not for long. On 1 January 1941 the 71st Pursuit Squadron (Interceptor) was activated at Selfridge Field and assigned to the 1st Pursuit Group (Interceptor) - a redesignation effective 6 December 1939. Despite folklore to the contrary, there is no evidence that the War Department chose the new squadron's designation by reversing the old squadron's number. The 94th provided the 71st's cadre, and the new squadron began training immediately. In the summer of 1941 it joined the group at the 1941 GHQ maneuvers in Louisiana and South Carolina.[86]

In July 1941 the 27th received the first models of the aircraft the 1st would take to war. The Lockheed P-38 Lightning "represented one of the most radical departures from tradition in American fighter development."[87] The Lightning featured a wing span of 52 feet and was 37

II - The Inter-War Years

feet 10 inches long. The P-26C the 94th took to Muroc in 1937 had a span of 28 feet and a length of 24 feet. The Lightning's two turbo-supercharged Allison V-1710s each produced 1,475 hp, giving the plane a top speed of 414 mph at 25,000 feet. The P-26, powered by a single 660 hp engine, attained a top speed of 234 mph at 7,500 feet. The Lightning carried four .50 caliber machine guns plus a 20mm cannon, the P-26 two .30 caliber or one .30 caliber and one .50 caliber machine guns.[88]

On 5 December 1941, Captain Ralph Garman led the air echelon of the 94th, consisting of twenty P-38s, to March Field, California, for what was to be a ninety-day temporary duty assignment. The 94th was at El Paso, Texas, when it heard about Pearl Harbor.[89]

Photo II-1

1st Pursuit Group emblem,
approved 21 January 1924

II - The Inter-War Years

Photo II-2

P-6E, 94th Pursuit Squadron
Note the Indian-head emblem, approved in place of the
hat-in-the-ring emblem on 6 September 1924.

Photo II-3

Boeing P-12E, 27th Pursuit Squadron

Photo II-4

Boeing P-26As, 95th Pursuit Squadron

Photo II-5

Consolidated PB-2A, 94th Pursuit Squadron

II - The Inter-War Years

Photo II-6

Seversky P-35, 27th Pursuit Squadron

Photo II-7

Curtiss P-36C, 27th Pursuit Squadron.
The unusual camoflage scheme was applied for tests
during the 1939 maneuvers.

Photo II-8
Boeing P-12Es in Stair Step Formation
27th Pursuit Squadron

Photo II-9

Curtiss P-6E, 27th Pursuit Squadron

Photo II-10

Curtiss P-6Es, 27th Pursuit Squadron

CHAPTER THREE

World War II

The 1st Pursuit Group was dispersed but otherwise ready for war on 7 December 1941. The 94th was at El Paso, Texas, with twenty P-38s, on its way to March Field, California. The remainder of the group, under Major Robert S. Israel, Jr., group commander, was at Selfridge. At 1800 on 7 December the group received a message from Headquarters, 1st Air Force, directing it to proceed to March Field. Group personnel stayed up all night preparing for the deployment, although the first echelon of support personnel did not leave Selfridge until 9 December. The 94th arrived at San Diego on 8 December; the 27th and the 71st, flying twelve P-38s and twenty-four P-43s, arrived two days later. The last contingent of group personnel left Selfridge on 12 December and the group reassembled on the 14th.[1]

Not long after its arrival on the West Coast, the 71st, in the process of converting to P-38s, adopted a unit emblem. The 27th, with its Falcon, and the 94th, with its Indian head, used traditional designs. The 71st adopted a more aggressive and flamboyant device. "In accordance with the motto of the 1st Pursuit Group" (conquer or die), the 71st chose:

> A bleached skull as the centerpiece of its insignia. The three yellow bolts, or flashes of lightning, represent the flights composing the squadron. Death, with red eyes and a gruesome smile, rides out of the clouds on three flashes of yellow, against a bright background of blue.[2]

The 71st used this emblem throughout the war, but not long after the end of the war the "Flying Fist" of the contemporary emblem replaced the death's head, reflecting an Air Force decision to do away with morbid characters in its unit emblems.

The group began 1942 with an assigned strength of 992 (81 officers and 911 enlisted), against an authorized strength of 1,260 (149 and 1,111, respectively). Newly assigned personnel increased unit strength, but the numbers gave no real sense of the situation. As the Air Corps expanded between 1939 and 1941, it often called upon the 1st Pursuit to provide cadres for new groups and squadrons. When the Air Corps organized new units after Pearl Harbor, it continued to use the 1st as a source of cadres, but on a much larger scale. On 3 January 1942 the group lost 124 men to the 51st Pursuit Group. On 1 February 129 more returned to Selfridge, where they became the core of the 80th Pursuit Group. Finally, on 25 April, as the group prepared to deploy to Europe, 474 enlisted men and 24 officers, including group commander Israel, since promoted to lieutenant colonel, were reassigned and formed the cadre of the 82d Pursuit Group. Morale and performance suffered as a result of these moves.[3]

The War Department recognized that the problems plaguing the 1st affected other units as well. In March 1942, General Henry H. Arnold, Chief, Army Air Forces (AAF), contacted Eddie Rickenbacker, recovering from injuries suffered in an airliner crash more than a year before. Arnold gave Rickenbacker a plane, a crew, and a mission: to visit flying units, "talk to these boys, inspire them, put some fire in them," and to look for reasons morale and performance seemed to be lagging throughout the United States.[4] Rickenbacker's tour began on 10 March 1942, and by his own count he visited forty-one groups in forty-one states in thirty-two days.[5]

Rickenbacker's travels took him to California, where he met with his old squadron, the 94th. The pilots assembled and, after giving them a pep talk that recalled the squadron's heritage, Rickenbacker asked the pilots to explain what was wrong. Their complaints ranged from bad food to limited flying time, a familiar litany Rickenbacker heard elsewhere on his tour. But one pilot voiced a complaint that Rickenbacker resolved to handle personally. Why, the pilot asked, was the 94th using the Indian head insignia? What had become of the hat-in-the-ring?[6]

On his return to Washington, Rickenbacker broached this and other questions to Arnold, who handled the easy one first: on 12 April 1942 he informed Rickenbacker that the hat-in-the-ring device would be reassigned to the 94th. The other problems Rickenbacker described to Arnold would not admit to such an easy solution. Rickenbacker placed the blame for the continuing morale problems not on the pilots -"There was nothing wrong with these boys. They were America's best: keen, alert, inspired, enthusiastic, fit. They craved action."[7] - but on the AAF itself, especially its maintenance and supply systems. As Rickenbacker saw it, the root cause of the morale problem was obvious: the pilots wanted to fly, but "the system" forced them to undergo "severely curtailed training. They wanted to give it all they had, but we were not letting them."[8]

> There was not enough equipment. It was not only a shortage of planes. The obstacles lay in the entire complex of maintenance .... There were not enough parts and equipment in inventory at any base I visited. Nor was there an efficient distribution system. Requisitions would go into supply and it might be days, even weeks, before the necessary part or parts arrived.... As a result, planes were grounded for weeks at a time for want of parts.[9]

General Arnold promised Rickenbacker that the AAF would try to deal with the problems he had uncovered. Events soon took care of complaints about a shortage of flying time.

As a result of strategic decisions made by the United States and Great Britain before the United States entered the war, America based its military strategy in the spring of 1942 on the notion that Germany posed a greater threat than Japan, and that the United States and its allies would, therefore, pursue a "Germany first" strategy. To implement this decision, the AAF developed plans to deploy a large part of its air strength to England. Planners aimed to have American air units in combat over Europe by mid-1942, with an eye toward an invasion of continental Europe in 1943. If, however, either the German or the Russian war efforts seemed near collapse, the air units could support an immediate cross-channel invasion in 1942. Both plans called for an accelerated build up of American aviation strength in England. The War Department dubbed the movement of AAF units to England in 1942 "Operation Bolero."[10]

The 1st Pursuit Group formed the vanguard of the Bolero buildup. On 23 April 1942, the War Department ordered continental commands to prepare various air units for overseas movement. The group received its alerting message on 29 April. Movement orders arrived on 14 May. They divided the group into two components. The air echelon consisted of eighty-five P-38Fs, a like number of pilots, a maintenance officer and sixty-five crew chiefs, an armament officer and five weapons specialists, and a communications officer and five radio and flight instruments specialists. These eighty-eight officers and seventy-five enlisted men moved by air throughout the deployment. Two flight surgeons and 200 additional enlisted men assigned to the air echelon made the initial movement across the United States by rail, but they flew on C-47 transports for the trans-Atlantic legs of the trip. The ground echelon, 99 officers and 872 enlisted men, moved from the United States to England by ship.[11]

The newly designated 1st Fighter Group (effective 15 May 1942) began its deployment to England on 17 May. Between then and 19 May, the air echelon left California for Dow Field, Maine. The ground echelon moved to Fort Dix, New Jersey. It arrived on 24 May and boarded the Queen Elizabeth on 3 June, where it joined the ground components of the 97th Bombardment, 31st Fighter, 60th Transport, and 5th Air Depot groups. The Queen Elizabeth sailed on 4 June and arrived at Gourock, Scotland, five days later. The ground echelon of the 1st Fighter Group then moved to an RAF station at Goxhill, England, where it settled in to await the arrival of the air echelon.[12]

The fighters had a more interesting time of it. By 25 May all three squadrons were at Dow, where they began training for the long flights ahead. The deployment from California afforded the group time to practice its long-distance, high-altitude formation flying, but during the stay in Maine the pilots continued to practice long formation flights. The Bolero deployment was to be a test: never before had the United States attempted to send fighters, even long-range, twin-engine aircraft like P-38s, on such a long over-water deployment in the face of uncertain weather conditions. The AAF believed that "the confidence of all pursuit pilots must be developed," so the group continued to fly progressively longer flights "to accustom pilots to the rigors of long hours in the air."[13] Official specifications on the P-38, used for planning the deployment, decreed that with 570 gallons of fuel, cruising at 15,000 feet at 200 knots, the P-38 could fly for six hours and still have fuel for at least an extra hour's flying left as a reserve. AAF planners used 1,443 miles as a safe maximum ferry range.[14]

Training progressed smoothly; the 1st Fighter Group had a great deal of experience with this type of operation. The transoceanic legs were scheduled to begin in early June, the exact date depending on the weather, but events half a world away forced a change in plans. The Battle of Midway loomed in the Pacific, and the War Department decided to move units to the West Coast to defend the region if the Japanese succeeded in their plan to smash the United States Pacific Fleet. The 1st Fighter Group therefore headed back toward California. It was at Morris Field, North Carolina, on 6 June when it learned that the Japanese fleet, minus four aircraft carriers, was in retreat in the Pacific. The group returned to Maine and began its Bolero deployment on 24 June.[15]

The trans-Atlantic ferry route comprised four legs. The route ran from Maine to Goose Bay, Labrador, thence to Greenland, Iceland, and Scotland. The group generally travelled in cells of five aircraft, with a B-17 escorting four P-38s. The rest of the air echelon moved in C-47s.[16]

The 1st Fighter Group began the Maine-Goose Bay leg on 24 June, with flights departing throughout the day. Airfields along the North Atlantic ferry route were primitive at this stage of the war. On arrival at Goose Bay, after a flight of about 600 miles, pilots found a single 1,500- by 150-foot gravel runway. Electric lights illuminated its southern edge, but spruce trees served as runway markers on the other edge and at the ends. Still, the group completed this leg without incident.[17]

The second leg presented greater challenges. The preferred route to Greenland took the aircraft from Goose Bay to "Bluie West One" (BW 1) Army Air Field, located on the northern shore of Tunugdliarfik fjord near Julianehaad, a distance of about 780 miles. Greenland's second field, Bluie West Eight, was judged "a superior location for aircraft operations," but it was almost 1,000 miles from Goose Bay. As the group moved eastward it used both BW 1 and BW 8.[18]

The third leg took the group to Reykjavik, Iceland. The 27th led the group into Iceland in early July, but the squadron did not make the move to Scotland for some months. The War Department ordered the 27th to remain in Iceland to help defend the island against German long-range patrol aircraft.[19] The first P-38s reached Prestwick, Scotland, on 9 July, when Colonel John N. Stone, the group commander, arrived with a flight of seven aircraft. The rest of the group remained strung out behind them. The evening of 10 July found forty-six P-38s at Goose Bay, eleven at BW 1, four at BW 8, and twelve in Iceland. By 14 July the total at Bluie West 1 reached fifty-seven P-38s, but on the same day bad weather forced six P-38s from the 94th and a B-17 down on the Greenland icecap as they departed on the Greenland-Iceland leg. Rescue units picked up all the crew members involved, and these six aircraft represented the group's only Bolero losses. The 31 July 1942 "Bolero Aircraft Status Report" placed the 1st Fighter Group "In England."[20]

Aircraft of the 1st Fighter Group moved to airfields near Hull, England, shortly after their arrival in Scotland. Group headquarters, the 71st, and the ground echelon of the 27th took up station at Goxhill, while the 94th moved to Kirton Lindsay. The air echelon of the 27th remained in Iceland where, on 14 August, one of its pilots participated in the destruction of the first German aircraft American pilots shot down in the European Theatre of Operations (ETO). Lieutenant Elza D. Shahan and Lieutenant Joseph D. Schafer of the 33d Fighter Squadron (P-40s) shared credit for the destruction of a FW-200 Condor, a four-engine reconnaissance aircraft.[21]

The 27th made its way from Iceland to the United Kingdom at the end of August, about the same time the VIIIth Fighter Command, Eighth Air Force, declared the 1st Fighter Group operational. Group strength at the time consisted of 129 officers and 1,060 enlisted men. It remained under the command of Colonel Stone. As of 1 September, the group headquarters was stationed with the 94th at Kirton Lindsay, the 27th at Colorne, and the 71st at Ibsley. On the same day Colonel Stone led thirty-two aircraft on a sweep over the French coast, the group's first World War II combat sorties over the continent. German pilots who rose to meet the group examined the P-38s from a respectful distance. Their reticence disappeared on later missions.[22]

The group received new identification letters and radio call-signs on 10 September 1942.

III - World War II

Aircraft of the 27th carried HV codes and pilots used "Petdog" as a call-sign. Those of the 71st sported LM codes, while the 94th used UN. The 71st used "Cragmore" as its call-sign, the 94th "Springcap."[23]

Although the 1st Fighter Group was back in the front lines, planners had trouble finding something for the unit to do. They knew the pilots lacked combat experience. Serious questions remained as to whether the P-38 could survive in combat with smaller, supposedly more nimble Bf-109s and FW-190s. Eighth Air Force operations officers were, therefore, reluctant to commit the group to fighter sweeps over the continent. American B-17s and B-24s raided heavily-defended continental targets, but the leaders of the bomber force still believed that the well-armed bombers could do the job without fighter escort. As a result, they opted not to use the Lightnings for bomber escort. Since the P-38 had been designed as an interceptor, the aircraft occasionally scrambled to meet German intruders over England, but these sorties resulted in few encounters, no victories, taught little about effective fighter tactics and doctrine, and provided no real opportunity for group pilots to gain combat experience.[24]

The group spent most of the summer of 1942 flying training missions and occasional fighter sweeps over France. Rickenbacker visited his old group in England in late September and early October. On 30 September he distributed "hat-in-the-ring" pins to the pilots of the 94th. Rickenbacker also met Major Alden B. Sherry, the group's intelligence officer. Sherry was an old friend, a member of the 94th Pursuit in World War I. He was the only man to serve in the group in both world wars. The War Diary of the 71st records that Rickenbacker watched the squadron take off on a mission on 2 October. The 71st and the group lost their first combat casualty on this mission, when Lieutenant William H. Young was shot down over a German airfield in France.[25]

When the group's ground echelon again packed up its equipment and boarded transports in England in late October, the rumor mills began working overtime. Speculation had the group going to France, to the Pacific, and even back to the United States. When the convoy cleared the Straits of Gibraltar on 6 November, the men of the 1st Fighter Group learned they were bound for North Africa. On 8 November the convoy dropped anchor in the Gulf of Oran. Group personnel began landing the next day. On 11 November a party of seven officers and 200 enlisted men established an advanced camp and airfield at Tafaroui, Algeria.[26]

The air echelon made the move to North Africa between 12-14 November. They completed the flight in two legs, with an interim stop at Gibraltar. The 27th led the way on 12 November and arrived at Tafaroui the next day, losing one pilot to mechanical difficulties over the Atlantic. The 71st made the flight without loss, but the 94th reported two pilots missing when it arrived at the new base. Captain James Harmon, the squadron commander, and Lieutenant Jack Ilfrey had both landed in Lisbon, where the neutral Portuguese showed every intention of holding the two Americans for the duration. Harmon talked the Portuguese into letting him go after he volunteered to leave his well-travelled P-38 behind as a souvenir. Ilfrey did even better than his commander: he talked his hosts into refueling his aircraft and removing the chocks from the wheels. Suitably serviced, he took off in front of his surprised guards.[27]

On 20 November the group dispersed to airfields behind the front. Group headquarters

As the ground campaign in North Africa progressed, the Germans and the Italians began an airlift to evacuate personnel from Africa to Italy and Sicily. The transport formations offered tempting targets to the group's fighters. On 5 April the group launched twenty-six aircraft on a sweep. With the 71st flying top cover, the 27th and the 94th attacked a large formation of transports escorted by fighters. The group claimed eleven Ju-52s, a Bf-109, and a Fiesler "Storch" destroyed, while the 27th lost two pilots. The 71st's turn came on 10 April, when it destroyed twenty Ju-52s, an FW-190, and an Italian fighter at no cost to itself. Group morale improved after these victories.[42] When the Germans resorted to other means to evacuate their forces, the group expanded its tactics. In late April the P-38s turned their attention to the freighters and barges moving out of Tunis and Bizerte, using dive and skip-bombing tactics to harry the fugitives. The North African campaign ended with the capture of Tunis on 7 May 1943.[43]

The end of the campaign brought the group a brief respite. While all three squadrons still flew weather reconnaissance, rescue escort, bomber escort, and ground attack sorties over the Mediterranean, Sicily, and Southern Italy, the hectic pace of the North African campaign gave way to a more relaxed schedule. On 1 August the 71st Fighter Squadron's diarist noted that: "We hope the whole month will be more like this. It's like something out of Mark Twain's Life on the Mississippi with nothing happening and the weather being ideal for lolling around and appreciating the virtues of taking life easy."[44]

The respite was brief. On 15 August, for example, the group launched sixty-one sorties. Twenty-four aircraft made dive-bombing attacks in southern Italy, twenty-nine P-38s escorted B-26s to Sapri, Italy, and eight more flew a search-and-rescue escort mission. Even this was only a prelude to the last week of the month. On 22 August the group's pilots began flying top-secret, low-level formation flights. The pilots apparently had some difficulty keeping their mouths shut; on 24 August the diarist of the 71st reported that all personnel were confined to base "because the word about all this secret practicing has leaked out." Support personnel knew that all three squadrons launched maximum-effort missions each day and that "everyone comes back looking like the cat that ate the canary."[45]

The group flew the well-rehearsed mission on 25 August. The target was the Foggia airfield complex in southern Italy. The 1st Fighter Group launched sixty-five aircraft under the command of Major George A. Rush, the group's operations officer, who flew as leader of the 71st's contingent. After joining up with eighty-five more P-38s from the 14th and 82nd Fighter Groups, the 150-plane formation proceeded at extremely low altitude to the target area 530 miles from base. The P-38s split into squadron-strength formations and hit eight airfields in the Foggia complex. The pilots "swept across the enemy fields, strafing the widely dispersed aircraft, gun positions, enemy troops, and other military targets."[46] During the attack, pilots of the 1st Fighter Group destroyed or damaged eighty-eight enemy aircraft, most on the ground, while the strike package as a whole claimed 150 aircraft destroyed or damaged.[47] The group lost two P-38s, one each from the 27th and the 71st, and these two squadrons each had one aircraft damaged.[48] The diarist of the 71st claimed that "for all the secret practicing and worrying, the mission was sure a floperoo as far as we were concerned."[49] The War Department thought differently: the 1st Fighter Group won its first Distinguished Unit Citation for this mission.[50]

III - World War II

The group won a second Distinguished Unit Citation on its next major mission. On 30 August the group launched a forty-four plane formation, led by Lieutenant Frank J. McIntosh of the 27th, to escort B-26s of the 319th and 320th Bombardment Groups to attack the railroad marshalling yard at Aversa, Italy. As the American formation crossed the Italian coast, 75-100 enemy fighters attacked it. The P-38s, outnumbered by at least two-to-one, met the defending fighters. During a forty-minute air battle the group destroyed eight, probably destroyed three, and damaged three more German aircraft, at a cost of thirteen missing. The bomber formation completed its work without interference and returned to base without a loss. The 71st called it "a bad show," but again the War Department disagreed. In 1946 the group received a DUC for its performance on this mission.[51]

In the meantime, Allied forces invaded Sicily on 9 July 1943. They cleared the island after a short land campaign during which the 1st Fighter Group flew air superiority, ground support, and interdiction missions. On 9 September 1943 American forces invaded Italy near Salerno, while Commonwealth forces landed in the heel of Italy. The group flew from a temporary airfield at Dittaino, Sicily, during the early days of the Italian campaign. Most pilots flew at least two sorties a day, and ground crews refuelled the aircraft from five-gallon cans. The stay in Sicily was temporary; the air echelon returned to a new station near Mateur on 18 September. There followed a series of station changes as the group moved closer to the advancing Italian front. On 5 October the air echelon moved from Mateur to Gambut, near Tobruk, Libya. Between 4-6 November the air echelon moved to airfields near Tunis. At about the same time the ground echelon moved to Monserrato airfield, Sardinia, to prepare for the arrival of the group's aircraft. The air echelon crossed to Monserrato on 29 November.[52]

Conditions at Monserrato were plush compared to those in North Africa. Pilots lived in a modern apartment house, unheated but otherwise palatial. Rooms were airy and comfortable, and morale soared. Group personnel had access to plenty of fresh food, bathing, and recreational facitlities. The brief idyl ended on 9 December, when the group moved to Gioia del Colle, near Bari in the heel of Italy.[53]

The group's morale improved by January 1944, but the supply situation had, if anything, deteriorated. On 4 January the group could muster only thirty-two operational aircraft. The buildup for the cross-channel invasion of France received higher priority, so the 1st, and most of the other units fighting in the Mediterranean, languished at the end of a long, tenuous, and inadequately fed supply line.[54]

On 8 January 1944 the group made the last of its many moves since late 1943. On that date both the air and ground echelons moved from Gioia del Colle to Salsola airfield, a former German base in the Foggia complex. Group headquarters remained at Salsola until February 1945, although the field flooded in the winter and was essentially abandoned from late fall through early spring. The sixty-mile-long complex of bases around Foggia became the home of the Fifteenth Air Force, organized on 1 November 1943. The 15th became the long-range, strategic bombing force in the Mediterranean theater, while the 12th became essentially a tactical air force.[55]

Despite the frequent moves and the shortage of aircraft, by late January 1944 the 1st Fighter Group had reached:

... a level of tactical proficiency higher than ever attained before. It flew smartly and competently, and handled itself professionally in the battle areas. There was an absence of landing and take-off accidents. Guns and sights seemed to work. Mostly, it seemed to have finally gotten a good estimate of the enemy. There was less confusion in a dogfight, and less panic by the flight and element leaders.[56]

One member of the group attributed the improvement to experience, better tactics (by now a four-flight, sixteen-plane formation was standard), and better pilots, who benefited from more instrument and gunnery training and better tactical training for the type of missions being flown.[57]

Newer aircraft, P-38Js, began arriving in the spring. On 16 April 1944, the group flew its 1,000th combat mission, when forty-eight P-38s escorted a force of B-24s to bomb Brasov, Rumania. This milestone drew less attention than a softball game played between the 27th and the 71st on 5 May. With $800 riding on the game, virtually the whole group turned out to watch the 71st beat the 27th 6-5.[58]

Aerial activity accelerated as the weather improved during the spring of 1944. The group earned another Distinguished Unit Citation for a mission on 18 May. The target for the heavy bombers that day was the Ploesti Romano-Americano Oil Refinery in Rumania. The 15th Air Force dispatched a force of about 700 bombers, but bad weather encountered en route to the target forced most to turn back. The 1st provided withdrawal cover for the bomber force. The fighters encountered the same bad weather that caused most of the bombers and their escorts to turn back, but the 1st Fighter Group's formation leader, Captain Walter F. Flynn of the 27th, decided to press on to the target area in case any of the bombers had gotten through. When the fighters arrived over the target, they found a force of about 140 bombers under attack by about eighty fighters, which had already destroyed six bombers. The forty-eight P-38s went to the aid of the bombers and pressed their attacks against the Germans until they drove them all off. The bombers returned to their bases without further losses. The 1st Fighter Group destroyed ten, probably destroyed three more, and damaged six German fighters at a cost of one P-38, whose pilot parachuted to safety en route to base.[59]

The group's next noteworthy mission was not nearly so successful. Again the target was the Ploesti Romano-Americano refinery. Heavy bombers had been unable to knock out this target, so 15th Air Force decided to attack it with fighter-bombers. The 82nd Fighter Group provided the fighter-bombers, thirty-six P-38s. The 1st Fighter Group provided cover for the 82d. The 1st launched thirty-nine aircraft, thirteen from each squadron. Like the Foggia raid, the attack formation approached the target at low altitude. In this case the defenders were waiting, and at least one hundred enemy aircraft intercepted the seventy-five P-38s.[60]

As the strike force neared the target, aircraft from the 82d moved into the lead, followed by those of the 94th, the 27th, and the 71st, which lagged about three miles behind the rest of the formation. Enemy fighters concentrated on the isolated 71st; by the time the 27th and the 94th could turn to help, the 71st had lost eight of its thirteen fighters. One 71st pilot, Lieutenant Herbert B. Hatch, shot down five of the attacking Germans on this mission, but his success did not make up for the losses (a ninth 71st plane went down on the way home). The rest of the American fighters fared little better; the 1st Fighter Group lost a total of fifteen

III - World War II

planes, while the 82d lost nine, or more than one-third of the strike package.[61] Captain William N. Richardson, the 71st Fighter Squadron's diarist, called this "the worst day in the history of the 71st Squadron."[62]

The remainder of 1944 proved less eventful. On 11 August the group deployed sixty aircraft to Corsica to support the allied invasion of Southern France (Operation Dragoon). During this deployment the group's highest scoring pilot, Lieutenant Thomas E. Maloney of the 27th (eight air-to-air kills), fell to flak. After crash landing in the Mediterranean, he floated to a French beach, which turned out to be mined, and injured both his legs when he set off one of the mines. He laid on the beach for ten days before a French farmer rescued him. Doctors saved his legs, and he was soon airlifted back to the United States.[63] On 15 December the group returned to the Foggia complex but landed at Lucera, ten miles west of Salsola.[64]

January 1945 proved a quiet month. Because of bad weather, the group flew on only eight days that month. The group's last major deployment began at the end of January, but the mission was an important one. During Operation Argonaut, the 1st Fighter Group escorted the British and American delegations to the Yalta Conference. The group deployed a total of sixty-one aircraft to Gibraltar, Oran, Malta, and eventually to Yalta itself. The deployment began on 28 January. From then until 4 February, the P-38s escorted the ships and planes carrying Franklin Roosevelt, Winston Churchill, and their aides eastward to the Crimea. The return voyage began on 11 February and ended on 21 February, when the distinguished travellers exited the Mediterranean. Returning P-38s went to Salsola, reoccupied in mid-February when the the runways dried out.[65]

As the war in Italy drew to a close, the 1st Fighter Group found itself flying more ground-attack missions. Losses to flak rose accordingly. On 31 March 1945 antiaircraft fire claimed Colonel Arthur C. Agan, 1st Fighter Group Commander, who became a prisoner of war. The group ranged over all of southern Europe and into Germany during the last days of the war. Lieutenant Warren Danielson of the 27th shot down an FW-190 on 15 April during a ground-attack mission to Passau and Regensburg, Germany, the group's last aerial kill of the war. Thus, to the 27th went the distinction of having shot down the group's first and last aerial victims. The group flew its last wartime mission on 6 May, when five P-38s from the 27th escorted two RAF bombers on a supply drop to Yugoslavia.[66]

Between 4 June 1942 and 6 May 1945 the 1st Fighter Group flew 20,955 sorties on 1,405 combat missions. The group scored 402.50 aerial kills: 27th - 176.50; 71st -102.00; 94th -124.00. The group also claimed 149 ground kills, 98 probables, and 231 damaged. The group lost 204 pilots killed or missing in action and twenty-eight pilots during training missions.[67] The group demobilized quickly at the end of the war. On 15 September 1945 what remained of the group moved to Caserta, near Naples. On 16 October 1945 the 1st Fighter Group was deactivated at Caserta, ending thirty-six years of continuous service to the nation.[68]

Photo III-1

Lockheed P-38 Lightning

III - World War II

Photo III-2

Well-travelled P-38 Lightning of the 27th Fighter Squadron, photographed in Italy in 1944.

Photo III-3

Lieutenant Herbert P. Hatch, 71st Fighter Squadron,
who downed five enemy aircraft on one mission in 1944.

III - World War II

Photo III-4

Preflight intelligence briefing.

Photo III-5
P-38 Lightnings of the 27th Fighter Squadron
Late 1944

CHAPTER FOUR

The Air Defense Era
1946 - 1969

As one of the Army Air Force's oldest combat units, it seemed only natural that military planners reserved a place for the 1st Fighter Group in the nation's postwar air arm. The 412th Fighter Group at March Field, California, was inactivated on 3 July 1946. Its personnel and equipment were assigned to the 1st Fighter Group, activated at March on the same date. At the time of its activation, the group's three squadrons (the 27th, 71st, and 94th Fighter Squadrons) flew P-80 Shooting Stars, America's first operational jet fighter. The group was further assigned to Twelfth Air Force and Tactical Air Command on 3 July.[1]

The next twenty-four years were a difficult time for the 1st Fighter Group. From July 1946 to February 1952 the group found itself attached to the newly organized 1st Fighter Wing, three numbered air forces, three regional air defense organizations, an air division, and four major commands. It experienced difficulty adjusting to the administrative changes caused by this organizational instability. The group also made three permanent changes of station and one temporary duty move during the same period and helped to introduce two new jet fighters, the F-80 and the F-86, into the Air Force's operational inventory. (The United States Air Force was established on 18 September 1947. The Air Force revised its fighter designation from "P" to "F" on 11 June 1948.) A new organizational scheme for the air defense forces led to the inactivation of both the wing and group headquarters in February 1952. The group headquarters was activated again in 1955, as was the wing headquarters the following year. The organizational situation stabilized after 1956, although the group was inactivated again in 1961. The wing went through another spate of organizational changes in 1969 and 1970, but by then forces were at work that would ultimately lead to the wing's return to the tactical air forces in 1970.

Few members of the 1st Fighter Group foresaw these difficulties in the summer of 1946 as they trained with their new jet fighters. The 412th had reported in the summer of 1945 that the P-80 would be well suited for bomber escort, counterair, and ground support. The 1st Fighter Group trained for these and other possible strategic and tactical missions. Pilot inexperience and mechanical difficulties combined to give the P-80 a high accident rate, while parts shortages curtailed operational training. Even so, the 1st Fighter Group maintained a heavy schedule of demonstration flights that served to introduce the fighter to a curious public.[2]

While the group carried out what were, for it, traditional operations that called to mind the unit's experiences between the two world wars, planners considered the peacetime organization of the Army Air Force. The group/squadron structure that had served well for years seemed suitable for operational units, but the experience of World War II suggested that the traditional approach to providing support to these operational organizations might prove less useful. A variety of "Base Units" provided a wide range of support services, but a divided chain of command created administrative and operational difficulties for both the flying units and the support organizations. In an effort to address these difficulties, Headquarters, Army Air Forces, issued AAF Regulation 20-15, "Reorganization of AAF Base Units and Installations," on 27 June 1947. This regulation, which laid out what became known as the

"Wing" or "Wing-Base" plan, prescribed a standard organizational setup for all Army Air Force bases worldwide. The plan called for the creation of a wing headquarters that established policy and supervised four functional groups: an operational group, an air base group, a maintenance and supply group, and a medical group. This plan offered better operational control and promised to provide improved mobility, since the wings were administratively, logistically, and operationally self-sufficient.[3]

The reorganization plan affected the 1st Fighter Group. The 1st Fighter Wing was activated at March Field and assigned to Twelfth Air Force and TAC on 15 August 1947. Headquarters, 1st Fighter Group and the 27th, 71st, and 94th Fighter Squadrons were assigned to the wing as its tactical component on the same date. The wing's subordinate maintenance, supply, and support organizations were also organized on 15 August. These included Headquarters, 1st Maintenance & Supply Group; Maintenance Squadron, 1st Maintenance & Supply Group; Supply Squadron, 1st Maintenance & Supply Group; and Headquarters and Headquarters Squadron, 1st Airdrome Group, with six component squadrons, designated A-F, which handled communications, security, civil engineering, food services, transportation, and base services. March Field was also the home of the 608th Aircraft Control & Warning Squadron, Headquarters, 506th Aircraft Control & Warning Group, and Headquarters, 67th Reconnaissance Group. These units were also assigned to the wing.[4]

In early April 1948, Headquarters, Twelfth Air Force issued a mission statement for the 1st Fighter Wing. Its complexity reflected both the wide range of the wing's responsibilities and the experimental nature of its work with new aircraft and new organizational forms. The mission statement directed the wing to:[5]

1. Prepare and assign missions to all units of the 1st Fighter Wing.

2. Attain and maintain the highest efficiency within the means available.

3. Maintain a highly mobile organization at all times.

4. Provide units for demonstration missions in accordance with directives from higher headquarters.

5. Cooperate with 12 AF, TAC, and other Air Force organizations in developing, testing, and improving the equipment, tactics, and techniques of fighter aviation.

6. Assume direct responsibility for units assigned or attached to the 1st Fighter Wing.

7. Aid in the development of air-ground cooperation techniques and doctrines, and to conduct training necessary for operation with ground and other Air Force units.

8. Provide units for active support of other commands for defense missions.

9. Prepare personnel designated by higher headquarters for overseas movement.

IV - The Air Defense Era

10. Conduct military training and perform special missions directed by higher headquarters.

11. Assist the recruiting program and in the separation of eligible personnel.

12. Keep higher headquarters informed of difficulties encountered and new developments in maintenance, operation, and training in currently assigned fighter aircraft.

The mission statement also noted that each individual assigned to the 1st Fighter Wing "should be thoroughly acquainted with the assigned mission and indoctrinated in such a manner that each person concerned feels that his portion of the task is a definite contribution to the accomplishment of the mission."[6]

The 1st Fighter Group's activities throughout the rest of 1948 reflected the many facets of this complex mission. On 1 April the 27th Fighter Squadron learned that it would deploy to Bergstrom Air Force Base, Texas, for tactical training with 2d Armored Division. The squadron was busy preparing for that trip when, on 27 April, group headquarters directed it to loan six of its P-80s, five pilots, and support equipment to the 71st Fighter Squadron, which had in the interval been directed to deploy to Spokane, Washington. The 27th feared that it would be unable to make its Texas deployment, but aircraft, pilots, and equipment borrowed from the 94th filled out the 27th's ranks in time for the flight to Bergstrom on 6 May. From 10-15 May the 27th flew air superiority, reconnaissance, and ground-support missions in conjunction with the 2d Armored.[7] From 16 August through 11 November the 1st Fighter Group deployed the 27th and 71st Fighter Squadrons to Eglin AFB, Florida, for a tactical test that involved some 8,500 men and five hundred aircraft. The 1st Fighter Group flew a variety of ground support and tactical demonstration flights. The 27th and the 71st flew F-80s; the 94th remained at March awaiting the arrival of its first F-86s.[8]

In December 1948 Twelfth Air Force was assigned from Tactical Air Command to Continental Air Command (ConAC), established on 1 December 1948. ConAC assumed jurisdiction over both TAC and the Air Defense Command (ADC). This move reflected an effort to concentrate all fighter forces deployed within the continental United States to strengthen the air defense of the North American continent. The move was largely an administrative convenience: the units assigned to ConAC were dual-trained and expected to revert to their primary strategic or tactical roles after the air defense battle was won. The 1st Fighter Wing was subsequently transferred from Twelfth Air Force/TAC to Fourth Air Force/ConAC on 20 December 1948.[9]

Organizational and equipment changes continued throughout 1949. The first F-86, assigned to the 94th Fighter Squadron, arrived on 15 February. By the end of June the wing had received seventy-nine of its eighty-three authorized F-86s. On 1 May the wing transferred from ConAC to Strategic Air Command (SAC) and the Fifteenth Air Force. The wing was subsequently attached to the 22d Bomb Wing on 1 July.[10]

While the wing stayed close to home because of a shortage of mounts for auxiliary fuel tanks and because so few bases were equipped to service the F-86, training and demonstration flights continued in the local area. Accidents plagued the flying units. These mishaps cost many aircraft and lives, but at least one pilot, Lieutenant Robert E. Farley of the 71st Fighter Squadron, gained a degree of notoriety from his misfortune. The squadron claimed that he became the first United States Air Force pilot to use an ejection seat during normal operations when he ejected from an out-of-control F-86 approximately 1,000 feet above the California desert. The new fighter developed numerous teething troubles during its first months of service, but 1st Fighter Group mechanics gradually overcame these difficulties. When the squadrons found themselves able to launch large formations on schedule, they competed to establish various formation records. The 71st struck first in September 1949, when it launched a twelve and later an eighteen-aircraft formation. The 27th and the 94th countered on 21 October. On that day the 94th launched three thirteen-plane formations, but the 27th topped this with two twenty-one plane formations. The purpose of this exercise became clear in early January 1950, when the 1st Fighter Group deployed a sizable contingent of aircraft to participate in the filming of the RKO film Jet Pilot. The group claimed a final formation record on 4 January when it passed a twenty-four plane formation (consisting of eight aircraft from each squadron) before the cameras.[11]

The 1st Fighter Group formed its own aerial demonstration team in January 1950. The team, dubbed the "Sabre Dancers," was composed of five members of the 27th Fighter Squadron. Captain Dwight S. Beckham flew lead, with Lieutenant Clement L. Bittner on left wing, Lieutenant Mervin M. Taylor in slot, and Lieutenant Russell E. Taliaferro on right wing. Taliaferro occasionally flew solo; in that case Lieutenant Robert W. McCormick moved to the wing position. The Sabre Dancers made what was probably their most widely viewed flight on 22 April 1950, when they performed before an Armed Forces Day audience at Eglin AFB, Florida, that included President Harry S. Truman, most of his Cabinet, and numerous other political leaders.[12]

After a winter notable only for a fire of suspicious origin that destroyed the group headquarters building on 25 February 1950, the wing embarked upon yet another series of organizational changes in the spring. Effective 16 April 1950 the 1st Fighter Wing was redesignated the 1st Fighter-Interceptor Wing, the same designation that was simultaneously applied to the group and its three squadrons. The wing had, some days previously, been relieved from its attachment to the 22d Bombardment Wing. Later that spring, Captains Richard D. Creighton of the 71st, Wyman D. Anderson of the 94th, and John D. Smith of the 27th shaved more than sixteen minutes off the San Francisco to Los Angeles aerial speed record on 20 May 1950, but it was something of a "last hurrah" for the early model F-86s the group was still flying. The group's F-86 fleet was grounded in June so that engineers and mechanics from the North American Aviation Company could complete a series of modifications designed to bring the F-86s up to the standards of later models.[13]

The organizational changes the wing had experienced since 1947 paled in comparison to the multitude of changes the unit underwent during the last six months of 1950. As of 30 June 1950, the 1st Fighter-Interceptor Group was assigned to the 1st Fighter-Interceptor Wing, which was itself assigned to Fifteenth Air Force and SAC. On 1 July the wing was relieved from assignment to Fifteenth Air Force and SAC and assigned to the Fourth Air Force and ConAC. Two days later the wing issued orders establishing advanced parties of its headquarters and component organizations at Victorville (later George) AFB, California:

IV - The Air Defense Era

Headquarters & HQ Squadron, 1st Fighter-Interceptor Wing

- Headquarters, 1st Fighter-Interceptor Group
-- 27th Fighter-Interceptor Squadron
-- 71st Fighter-Interceptor Squadron
-- 94th Fighter-Interceptor Squadron

- Headquarters, 1st Maintenance & Support Group
-- 1st Support Squadron
-- 1st Maintenance Squadron
-- 1st Motor Vehicle Squadron

- Headquarters & HQ Squadron, 1st Air Base Group
-- 1st Communications Squadron
-- 1st Air Police Squadron
-- 1st Installations Squadron
-- 1st Food Service Squadron

- 1st Medical Group

The wing made its permanent change of station move to Victorville on 18 July. On 22 July an advanced party of personnel from Headquarters, 1st Fighter-Interceptor Group and the 27th and 71st Fighter-Interceptor Squadrons departed for Griffiss AFB, New York. A letter directing the wing to send the group headquarters and the 27th and the 71st to Griffiss for attachment to the Eastern Air Defense Force (EADF), ConAC, arrived on 30 July. Headquarters, 1st Fighter-Interceptor Wing and the 94th Fighter-Interceptor Squadron were assigned to the Western Air Defense Force, ConAC, on 1 August, while the group headquarters and the 27th and 71st were attached to the EADF on 15 August. The wing was attached to the 27th Air Division, WADF, on 20 September. Finally, one month later, the 71st Fighter-Interceptor Squadron moved from Griffiss AFB to Pittsburgh International Airport, Pennsylvania. As of 31 December 1950 Headquarters, 1st Fighter-Interceptor Wing and the 94th were stationed at George AFB, assigned to the WADF, and attached to the 27th Air Division. Headquarters, 1st Fighter-Interceptor Group, while still assigned to the wing, was stationed at Griffiss AFB with the 27th. The 71st was at Pittsburgh. The units on the East Coast were attached to the EADF.[14]

Changes continued throughout 1951. Air Defense Command was reestablished as a major command on 1 January 1951. Continental Air Command lost responsibility for air defense on that date, and the wing was assigned to ADC. In May, the 27th and the 71st were attached to the 103d Fighter-Interceptor Wing, which provided administrative and logistical support and operational control, although the squadrons remained assigned to the 1st Fighter Group. Headquarters, 1st Fighter Group was relieved from attachment to the Eastern Air Defense Force and moved from Griffiss to George (with a strength of two officers and two enlisted men) on 4 June. Meanwhile, at George AFB, the 188th Fighter-Interceptor Squadron was attached to the 1st Fighter-Interceptor Wing, which provided administrative support and operational control.[15]

Air Defense Command planners recognized that the policy of deploying squadrons over a wide area negated whatever advantages may have accrued from the establishment of the wing-base plan in 1948. In the case of the 1st Fighter-Interceptor Wing, a wing headquarters stationed in California could provide only limited control and virtually no support to a group headquarters and squadrons deployed on the East Coast. While the policy of attaching units to higher headquarters established an ad hoc means of supplying the needed support, it was a cumbersome procedure that blurred organizational lines and did nothing for morale or unit cohesion above the squadron level. While staff officers at the Air Force level still believed that the wing-base plan was central to maintaining tactical mobility, the Air Defense Command staff argued that the need to disperse its air defense squadrons made wing and even group headquarters unnecessary and manpower-expensive organizational levels. The wing's days were numbered.[16]

With the exception of the Headquarters and Headquarters Squadron, and the three fighter-interceptor squadrons, all 1st Fighter-Interceptor Wing organizations and the group headquarters were reduced to a strength of one officer and one enlisted man on 30 November 1951, at which time the wing moved from George Air Force Base, California, to Norton Air Force Base, California. On 2 February 1952, Headquarters, Air Defense Command relieved the operational squadrons from their existing assignments and attachments and assigned them to newly organized "defense wings": the 27th to the 4711th Air Defense Wing (ADW), Eastern Air Defense Force, the 71st to the 4708th ADW, EADF, and the 94th to the 4705th ADW, WADF. Headquarters, Air Defense Command inactivated the 1st Fighter-Interceptor Wing and the 1st Fighter-Interceptor Group on 6 February 1952.[17]

The organizational instability of the early 1950s was rooted in the demands of the Korean War. Faced with the need to spread its squadrons out to cover the nation as other units deployed to the Pacific, air defense planners devised new organizational plans to enable the units to fulfill their missions without tying up unacceptably large numbers of personnel in what appeared to be superfluous command levels and support organizations. The "Air Defense Wings" created to replace operational headquarters were administrative and logistics support organizations which supervised squadrons over a wide geographic area. The squadrons were operationally responsible to regional air defense forces and control centers. With the end of the war in Korea the Air Defense Command found itself in a position to return to a more traditional command structure. On 20 June 1955 the 1st Fighter-Interceptor Group was redesignated the 1st Fighter Group (Air Defense). It was activated and assigned to the 4708th Air Defense Wing, Eastern Air Defense Force, Air Defense Command, at Selfridge AFB, Michigan. The 71st and the 94th Fighter-Interceptor Squadrons were assigned to the group; the 27th remained at Griffiss, assigned to the 4711th Air Defense Wing, Eastern Air Defense Force. The 1st Fighter-Interceptor Wing was redesignated the 1st Fighter Wing (Air Defense) on 14 September 1956 and activated on 18 October 1956 with the 1st Fighter Group (Air Defense) assigned. Other units assigned to the wing at that time included the 1st Maintenance & Supply Group (1st Supply Squadron, 1st Field Maintenance Squadron, and 1st Transportation Squadron assigned), the 1st Air Base Group (1st Air Police Squadron, 1st Operations Squadron, 1st Food Service Squadron, 1st Installations Squadron, and the 1st Women's Air Force Squadron Section assigned), and the 1st USAF Hospital.[18]

After enduring a six-year period of frequent organizational changes, the wing began a period of stability in 1957. For approximately the next thirteen years it remained at Selfridge

IV - The Air Defense Era

AFB, serving as part of the 30th Air Division and, after 1 April 1959, the Detroit Air Defense Sector, all part of Air Defense Command. Both the 71st and the 94th traded their F-86s for F-102 Delta Dagger interceptors between 1958 and 1960.[19]

A major reorganization of wing control and support functions occurred on 1 February 1961. In the most significant change, a newly established wing Deputy Commander for Operations and his staff assumed the functions and responsibilities of the old fighter group headquarters, which was inactivated. The flying squadrons thereafter reported directly to the wing through the operations staff.[20]

Maintenance and support activities were reorganized as well. Three maintenance squadrons - the 1st Field Maintenance Squadron, 1st Organizational Maintenance Squadron, and the 1st Armament & Electronics Maintenance Squadron (activated on 17 October 1958 to replace the 1st Consolidated Aircraft Maintenance Squadron) reported to the wing through a Deputy Commander for Maintenance. The 1st Air Base Group supported operations through the 1st Air Police, Civil Engineering, Combat Support, Supply, and Transportation squadrons.[21]

While the wing and its units operated from Selfridge AFB, Michigan, the 27th Fighter-Interceptor Squadron remained on the east coast. As of 31 December 1961 it was stationed at Bangor, Maine, and assigned to the Bangor Air Defense Sector, 26th Air Division. At that time the squadron was equipped with F-106 Delta Darts.[22]

In October 1962 the wing responded to the Cuban Missile Crisis by deploying aircraft, support personnel, equipment and supplies to Patrick Air Force Base, Florida, and Volk Field, Wisconsin. From 19 October through 27 November wing aircraft flew 620 sorties and 1,274 hours, most from Patrick AFB, while maintaining a mission-ready rate of approximately eighty percent.[23] Wing life reverted to more normal training routines at year's end, and the pattern continued through 1963 and 1964. Only one noteworthy organizational change occurred during those years: on 1 April 1963, the 1st Air Base Group was redesignated the 1st Combat Support Group.[24] In April 1964 a detachment of the 71st deployed to Elmendorf AFB, Alaska, was shaken by the earthquake that rocked the state. A tornado struck the Capehart military housing area at Selfridge in May 1964, killing four military dependents.[25]

Beginning in about 1965 the wing began to transfer pilots to other units in or en route to Vietnam. While the wing itself did not participate in the war, its units were soon manned by personnel who had completed tours in Southeast Asia. Wing dining-ins held periodically for the rest of the decade invariably featured a presentation ceremony where personnel received various awards and commendations they had earned overseas.[26]

Organizational changes continued to whittle away at the wing's strength in 1966 and 1967. The wing was assigned to the 34th Air Division, First Air Force, on 1 April 1966. In September the 1st Armament & Electronics Maintenance Squadron was organized into two squadrons, the 1st Communications & Electronics Maintenance Squadron and the 1st Munitions Maintenance Squadron. This organization changed again on 16 January 1967, when the 71st Fighter-Interceptor Squadron, which had won top prize in the F-106 category at the 1965 William Tell weapons competition at Tyndall AFB, Florida, was transferred to the 328th

Fighter Wing (Air Defense), Tenth Air Force, at Richards-Gebauer Air Force Base, Missouri. This reorganization left the 1st Fighter Wing (Air Defense), with only one fighter squadron, the 94th.[27]

This reduced alignment made the existing four-squadron maintenance organization unnecessary. On 16 January 1967 the 1st Communications & Electronics Maintenance Squadron, the 1st Field Maintenance Squadron, the 1st Organizational Maintenance Squadron, and the 1st Munitions Maintenance Squadron were inactivated and their functions assigned to the newly-activated 1st Consolidated Aircraft Maintenance Squadron. By the end of March 1967, the wing was little more than a shadow of its former self. Headquarters, 1st Fighter Wing (Air Defense), supervised the operations of its assigned units through the offices of two deputy commanders (materiel and operations) and the commander of the combat support group. The 94th Fighter-Interceptor Squadron, which mustered seventeen single-seat F-106As, two two-seat F-106B trainers, and seven T-33 trainers, reported to the Deputy Commander for Operations. The Deputy Commander for Materiel (formerly Deputy Commander for Maintenance) controlled the 1st Consolidated Maintenance Squadron. The 1st Combat Support Group consisted of the 1st Civil Engineering, 1st Supply, 1st Transportation, and 1st Air Police Squadrons, plus a Headquarters Squadron Section and a Women's Air Force Squadron. The 1st USAF Hospital was also assigned to the wing. The 71st Fighter-Interceptor Squadron was assigned to the 328th Fighter Wing (Air Defense), 30th Air Division, First Air Force, at Richards-Geubauer AFB, Missouri. The 27th was at Bangor, Maine, assigned to the 36th Air Division, 1st Air Force.[28]

The reduced wing stayed busy. From 24 July through 4 August 1967 Selfridge became the hub of federal activities mobilized during riots in Detroit. Elements of the 3d Brigade, 82d Airborne Division and the 2d Brigade, 101st Airborne Division, a total of some 12,000 combat and support personnel, eventually passed through the base. From 1500 on 24 July to 1500 the next day, the base received 4,700 troops and 1,008 tons of cargo. On 1 August the base handled 363 C-130 sorties, 6,036 troops, and 2,492 tons of cargo. By the time the tactical command post at Selfridge was closed at 1130 on 4 August, the base had processed 1,389 C-130 sorties, 12,058 troops, and 4,735.6 tons of cargo.[29]

In September 1968 the 71st Fighter-Interceptor Squadron was relieved from assignment to the 328th Fighter Wing (Air Defense) at Richards-Gebauer AFB, Missouri, and transferred to the 28th Air Division, Tenth Air Force, at Malmstrom AFB, Montana, where it became a self-contained unit operating on the SAC base. Between 20 May and 5 November 1969, the 94th deployed to Osan Air Base, Korea, for exercise College Cadence. It was to be the 1st Fighter Wing's last major air defense effort.[30]

On 1 December 1969 the 94th was transferred to Wurtsmith AFB, Michigan, (the old 1st Pursuit Group's Oscoda training camp, now put to other uses) pending the inactivation of the 1st Fighter Wing, which was assigned to the 23d Air Division on that date. On 31 December 1969 the wing, with no units under its control, transferred to Hamilton AFB, California, and was assigned to the 26th Air Division. The 1st Combat Support Group and its component squadrons were inactivated; personnel and equipment were transferred to the 4708th Air Base Group, 23d Air Division, at Duluth International Airport, Minnesota, on 1 January 1970.[31]

IV - The Air Defense Era

Although the designation remained the same, the 1st Fighter Wing was barely recognizable as a descendant of the 1st Pursuit. The three fighter squadrons were scattered from Maine to Michigan to Montana. The support organizations were inactive. Moves were underway, however, that would see the "old" 1st Fighter Wing reassembled before the year was out.

IV - The Air Defense Era

Photo IV-1

Lockhead P-80's, 71st Fighter Squadron

IV - The Air Defense Era

Photo IV-2

North American F-86D, 94th Fighter-Interceptor Squadron

Photo IV-3

Convair F-102, 71st Fighter-Interceptor Squadron

IV - The Air Defense Era

Photo IV-4

Convair F-106, 94th Fighter-Interceptor Squadron

Photo IV-5

North American F-86s, 27th Fighter-Interceptor Squadron

Photo IV-6

North American F-86D, 71st Fighter-Interceptor Squadron

CHAPTER FIVE

Back to TAC, 1970 - 1983

On 1 August 1968, General William W. Momyer became commander of Tactical Air Command. While he devoted most of his attention to the pressing problems the command faced during the war in Vietnam, General Momyer also concerned himself with the designation of the units under his command. The movement of units to and from Vietnam left TAC with a mixed force. Some of its organizations had long and honorable tactical traditions. Others used four-digit, command-controlled designations that gave them no history or traditions. General Momyer therefore directed the TAC planning staff to replace the four-digit designations with those of units that had a combat record dating from either World War II or Korea. He also directed the staff to "retain illustrious [Air Force controlled] designators for the active tactical forces." This policy, plus the training demands caused by the war in Vietnam, led to the 1st Fighter Wing's return to TAC in October 1970.[1]

Headquarters, United States Air Force authorized the reassignment of the 1st Fighter Wing (Air Defense) from Aerospace Defense Command to Tactical Air Command on 30 July 1970. Three days later, HQ ADC directed the commander of the 26th Air Division to move Headquarters, 1st Fighter Wing (Air Defense); Headquarters, 1st Combat Support Group; the 1st Security Police, 1st Civil Engineering, 1st Transportation, and 1st Supply Squadrons; and the 1st USAF Hospital from Hamilton AFB, California, to MacDill AFB, Florida. All units moved without personnel or equipment. The units were reassigned from ADC to TAC when they arrived at MacDill.[2]

The 15th Tactical Fighter Wing at MacDill provided personnel and equipment to TAC's newest wing. Four major changes occurred at the Florida base on 1 October 1970.

- HQ TAC redesignated two organizations. Headquarters, 1st Fighter Wing (Air Defense) was redesignated Headquarters, 1st Tactical Fighter Wing, and the 1st USAF Hospital was redesignated 1st Tactical Hospital.

- The command inactivated HQ 15th TFW. HQ 1st TFW "absorbed" its personnel and equipment. In a similar manner, units of the 1st TFW absorbed the personnel and equipment of Headquarters, 15th Combat Support Group; the 15th Supply, Civil Engineering, Services, Transportation, and Security Police Squadrons; and the 15th Tactical Hospital.

- HQ TAC activated the 1st Services Squadron and assigned it to the 1st Combat Support Group at MacDill. It also activated the 1st Combat Support Squadron, stationed it at Avon Park Range, Florida, and assigned it to the 1st CSG.

- HQ TAC relieved three support organizations and five flying squadrons from assignment to the 15th TFW and assigned them to the 1st TFW. The support organizations included the 15th Field Maintenance Squadron, the 589th Air Force Band (assigned to the 1st CSG), and the USAF Regional Hospital, MacDill. The flying squadrons were the 45th, 46th, and 47th Tactical Fighter Squadrons (equipped with F-4 Phantom IIs), the 4530th Tactical Training Squadron (also equipped with F-4s), and the 4424th Combat Crew Training Squadron (equipped with B-57 Canberra bombers).

Finally, the command assigned the wing to the 836th Air Division. The 1st Tactical Fighter Wing assumed its place as one of TAC's frontline fighter units.[3]

The 4th Tactical Fighter Wing, a TAC unit of long standing, with a distinguished history of its own that dated back to 1942, noted the 1st TFW's return to TAC. The 4th announced that it was

> ... pleased to welcome the 1 TFW into the TAC family. We are cognizant of your illustrious history and the tradition you established while conducting intercept training. We trust that your performance will continue in the same exemplary manner when you commence fighter operations . . . . The 4th TFW has been first in TAC for too long to be aware of the relative ratings of other wings, but we are sure you will find the competition for second stimulating and (hopefully) rewarding.[4]

The 4th TFW signed the greeting with its motto, "Fourth But First." The 1st TFW did not ignore the challenge:

> Reference 4 TFW message . . . your kind remarks are appreciated, as well as the pathos and poignancy which mark your understandable longing for first place. However, we feel constrained to remind you that neither assertion nor ambition alone can grant position.[5]

The wing signed its message "First, as acknowledged."

The friendly conflict between the 1st and the 4th, both F-4 units, never developed. On 23 December 1970, TAC revised the primary mission of the 1st TFW from that of an operational wing to that of a replacement training unit (RTU). The war in Vietnam had strained TAC training assets, so the command decided that it needed to convert a line unit to augment its training program. The command selected the 1st because the climate and range facilities in the MacDill area (Tampa, Florida) were ideal for the type of flying involved. Colonel Travis R. McNeil, wing commander, concerned that the relegation to RTU status might affect morale, reminded wing personnel that "although in some ways it would seem that the First should be an operational unit, we . . . must approach it in the light that you go to the First and the best when you need help, as TAC does. We can do anything we are tasked to do."[6]

The mission change involved a fundamental shift in the wing's operational responsibilities. A TAC operational fighter wing had a two-fold mission in the early 1970's. Its primary mission was:

> To execute tactical fighter missions designed to destroy enemy military forces, supplies, equipment, communications systems, and installations with nuclear or conventional weapons. Engage and destroy enemy air forces in either an offensive or defensive role by visual interception, airborne radar, or air control and warning

V - Back to TAC

systems.

The second element of the mission statement directed the operational wing "to provide replacement training of combat aircrews and tactical maintenance personnel in accordance with prescribed syllabi and directives."[7]

The mission of the command's replacement training units was more simple: "to provide combat crew training for aircrew personnel of the US military forces and selected allied military services as determined by Headquarters USAF and directed by Headquarters Tactical Air Command."[8] The mission statement applied to the wing's squadrons shed more light on what the wing's overall mission entailed and introduced a secondary role for units primarily devoted to replacement training. The command directed the squadrons to, first, "conduct combat aircrew academic and flight training in the tactics, techniques, and operations of assigned aircraft and associated equipment," and second, to "maintain a state of readiness of personnel and equipment for dispersal and/or augmentation of tactical forces as directed."[9] The 1st Tactical Fighter Wing fulfilled both parts of this mission during the almost five years it was active at MacDill.

The last step in General Momyer's program to reconstitute historic tactical units, at least as far as it concerned the 1st Tactical Fighter Wing, came in May 1971. The commanders of the 45th, 46th, and 47th Tactical Fighter Squadrons participated in a "shootout" at the Avon Park Gunnery Range on 14 May. The command had decided that the designations of the 27th, 71st, and 94th fighter squadrons would be reassigned to the 1st Tactical Fighter Wing. The shootout determined the assignment of the historic designations among the wing's three squadrons. Lieutenant Colonel Donald W. Martin, commander of the 47th Tactical Fighter Squadron, scored 113 out of 126 possible points and chose the 94th designation. Lieutenant Colonel David O. Walsh of the 46th finished second; the 46th opted for the 27th. This left the 71st's designation for the 45 TFS. The redesignations became effective on 1 July 1971, when HQ TAC inactivated the 45th, 46th, and 47th Tactical Fighter Squadrons. Their assets transferred to the newly activated 27th, 71st, and 94th Tactical Fighter Squadrons. Another organizational change effective 1 July 1971 transferred the wing from the 836th Air Division, inactivated on that date, to Ninth Air Force.[10]

By July 1971, the 1st Tactical Fighter Wing had reverted to an organization that recalled the 1st Pursuit Group of earlier days. The wing spent the next four years providing advanced tactical training to F-4 and B-57 aircrews, most of whom later saw service in Vietnam. On 1 October 1971, HQ TAC inactivated the 4530th Tactical Training Squadron, which, in addition to other duties, had trained Australian F-4 aircrew members and maintenance personnel during project Peace Reef. The 4501st Tactical Fighter Replacement Squadron, equipped with F-4s, assumed the 4530th's place in the wing's structure on the same date. The command inactivated the 4424th Combat Crew Training Squadron, the wing's B-57 training unit, on 30 June 1972, leaving the wing with four flying squadrons. All conducted advanced F-4 tactical training.[11]

Although it seems unlikely that many people in the 1st TFW were aware of them, discussions underway between HQ TAC and HQ USAF in the spring of 1972 were destined to have a significant impact on the wing's future. McDonnell-Douglas Aircraft Company rolled out the first YF-15 Eagle at its St Louis plant on 26 June 1972. About six weeks before, on 2 May 1972, General Momyer had decided that TAC would base its first F-15 wing at Langley AFB, Virginia. When he asked Air Force Chief of Staff General John D. Ryan to approve this decision, General Momyer noted that Langley, the home of HQ TAC since 1946, was a "traditional home of tactical fighters." He also suggested that Langley's location (near Hampton in southeastern Virginia) provided "an advantageous geographic position for TAC's secondary air defense mission of the eastern United States." It was also an "optimum... location" for European deployments, while an existing overwater range fifty nautical miles southeast of Langley offered suitable training areas with "minimum operational constraints and ecological impacts."[12]

On 14 March 1974, HQ USAF announced its plans to station the Air Force's first operational F-15 wing at Langley. (The first F-15 unit, the 58th Tactical Fighter Training Wing, was stationed at Luke AFB, Arizona.) Neither the Air Force nor TAC had selected a unit to assume this responsibility, so the TAC planning staff began to examine possible candidates. Working from historical research done in 1970 which "identified and ranked fighter wings by historic illustriousness," the planners generated a list of eight possible units. The 1st TFW ranked first, followed by the 4th, 31st, 49th, and 35th TFWs, the 56th Special Operations Wing, and the 347th and 388th TFWs. The top five were already active units, so on 4 April 1974, Brigadier General Jesse M. Allen, TAC Deputy Chief of Staff, Plans, asked the HQ USAF programming staff to assign the 56th TFW designation and the designations of its three original squadrons, the 61st, 62d, and 63d TFSs, to the F-15 wing slated to be activated at Langley in 1976.[13]

After more than a year of deliberation and discussion, the Air Force staff turned down the TAC request. On 14 May 1975 HQ USAF directed the Pacific Air Forces (PACAF) staff to move the 56th SOW from Nakhon Phanom Airport, Thailand, to MacDill AFB, Florida. The Air Staff had decided that TAC's most historic unit would become the Air Force's first operational F-15 wing.[14]

On 22 May 1975, HQ PACAF directed the movement of the 56th SOW from Thailand to MacDill, without personnel or equipment, effective 30 June. On 6 June, HQ TAC directed Ninth Air Force to move HQ 1st TFW; the 27th, 71st, and 94th TFSs; and the 1st Avionics Maintenance, Field Maintenance, Munitions Maintenance, and Organizational Maintenance Squadrons (in active status but without personnel or equipment), from MacDill to Langley, effective 30 June 1975. On that day the organizations at MacDill underwent a series of changes not unlike those experienced on 1 October 1970:

- HQ TAC assigned the 56th SOW to Ninth Air Force.

- The command redesignated the 56th SOW the 56th Tactical Fighter Wing.

- The command activated two tactical fighter (61st and 63d) and four support (56th Avionics Maintenance, 56th Field Maintenance, 56th Munitions Maintenance, and 56th Organizational Maintenance) squadrons at MacDill and assigned them to the 56th TFW.

V - Back to TAC

- HQ TAC assigned the USAF Regional Hospital, MacDill, the 4501st Tactical Fighter Replacement Squadron, the 56th Combat Support Group, the 56th Supply Squadron, and the 56th Transportation Squadrons to the 56th TFW.

- HQ TAC assigned the 56th Civil Engineering Squadron and the 56th Security Police Squadron to the 56th Combat Support Group. It activated the 56th Services Squadron and assigned it to the 56th CSG at MacDill. It also activated the 56th Combat Support Squadron at Avon Park Range, Florida, and assigned it to the 56th CSG.

- The command redesignated the 62d Fighter Interceptor Training Squadron the 62d Tactical Fighter Squadron and assigned it to the 56th TFW.

As the command assembled the 56th TFW, it completed the temporary break up of the 1st TFW. On 30 June 1975, HQ TAC inactivated HQ 1st CSG, and the 1st Transportation, Supply, Civil Engineering, Security Police, and Services Squadrons at MacDill and the 1st Combat Support Squadron at Avon Park Range, Florida. The organizations activated at MacDill on 30 June absorbed the personnel and equipment of the 1st TFW organizations either inactivated at or moved from MacDill at that time.[15]

To review the changes briefly, 1 July 1975 found the 1st Tactical Fighter Wing and its operational and maintenance squadrons at Langley Air Force Base, Virginia, represented by a five-member cadre under Lieutenant Colonel George H. Miller. The 4500th Air Base Wing at Langley provided support services to the newly arrived wing. The personnel and equipment the 1st TFW left behind at MacDill belonged to the 56th Tactical Fighter Wing. Headquarters, 1st Combat Support Group and its component squadrons were temporarily inactive.

Wing personnel worked for the next six months to prepare facilities at Langley and to learn the skills necessary to bring the wing to fully operational status. Pilots selected to fly the F-15 completed conversion training at Luke AFB, Arizona, while the command built the wing's maintenance squadrons up to strength with personnel trained to support the aircraft. The wing, now under the command of Brigadier General Larry D. Welch, demonstrated flexibility and resilience in its response to the construction, maintenance, operational, and training problems that developed, and by the end of 1975 Langley was ready to begin receiving its Eagles. Lieutenant Colonel John Britt, operations officer of the 27th Tactical Fighter Squadron, flew aircraft 74-0137, a two-seat TF-15 (later designated F-15B), into Langley on 18 December 1975. The official welcoming ceremonies, dubbed "Eagle Day," were not held until 9 January 1976, when Lieutenant Colonel Larry Craft, commander of the 27th, arrived with a single-seat F-15, 74-0083. Aircraft and aircrews arriving throughout 1976, at a programmed rate of eight aircraft per month, enabled the wing to build toward its authorized strength of seventy-two aircraft in three twenty-four plane squadrons. The 27th Tactical Fighter Squadron became operationally ready in the F-15 in October 1976. The 71st TFS reached that status in December 1976. In recognition of its accomplishments in introducing the F-15 into the inventory, the United States Air Force, on 1 March 1978, awarded the 1st Tactical Fighter Wing the Air Force Outstanding Unit Award for "exceptionally meritorious service" from 1 July 1975 to 31 October 1976.[16]

This left the 94th as the wing's only squadron not yet operationally ready. Both HQ TAC and the wing anticipated this situation, because once the first two squadron's reached operational status, the TAC pilot training pipeline and the wing and its organizations shifted gears to support operation Ready Eagle, a Tactical Air Command/United States Air Forces in Europe (USAFE) program to provide USAFE with its first operationally ready F-15 wing in the shortest possible time. The USAFE wing selected to transition to the F-15, the 36th Tactical Fighter Wing, stationed at Bitburg Air Base, Germany, established an operating location at Langley to oversee the maintenance and operations training provided by 1st TFW organizations augmented for that purpose. The 1st provided the 36th with eighty-eight operationally ready pilots and 522 maintenance specialists, who later trained an additional 1,100 maintenance personnel at Bitburg. The Ready Eagle schedule called for the 36th to deploy its first squadron to Germany by 15 April 1977, its third by 30 September. The first squadron actually deployed on 27 April and Ready Eagle was completed by 23 September, when the last European-bound F-15s left Langley. The 94th then completed its build-up toward operationally ready status, reaching that point by December 1977. By the end of 1977, then, the 1st Tactical Fighter Wing had completed its own transition to a new aircraft while simultaneously providing advanced tactical training for a second F-15 wing.[17]

Organizational changes continued in the interim. On 19 April 1976, HQ TAC relieved the 6th Airborne Command and Control Squadron, which flew Boeing EC-135 airborne command posts in support of the Commander-in-Chief, Atlantic Command, from its assignment to the 4500th Air Base Wing and assigned it to the 1st TFW. A year later, on 15 April 1977, the command activated Headquarters, 1st Combat Support Group, and the 1st Services, 1st Supply, 1st Civil Engineering, 1st Security Police, and 1st Transportation Squadrons at Langley. Personnel assigned to the newly activated squadrons came from 4500th ABW organizations inactivated on the same date. The 1st TFW became the host unit at Langley Air Force Base with the inactivation of the 4500th ABW.[18]

Mobility became a cornerstone of the wing's mission as it built up its F-15 strength. Tactical Air Command mission regulations directed the wing to prepare to deploy and operate its aircraft from locations worldwide. As the Air Force's first F-15 wing, the 1st TFW found itself called upon to demonstrate its ability to deploy forces almost as soon as the wing had the required number of aircraft on hand. The 27th Tactical Fighter Squadron, for example, deployed eight aircraft to Nellis AFB, Nevada, for Red Flag VI on 6 July 1976, only seventeen days after the squadron had received its twenty-fourth aircraft.[19]

HQ TAC levied these demanding requirements on the wing for several reasons. The command wished to expand both the wing's and the command's tactical training base by introducing its most advanced aircraft into its most realistic training environment. The wing enjoyed the opportunity to conduct its training in a challenging training arena. Furthermore, both the command and the wing used the deployments to test, the F-15 support system in a demanding yet controlled operational environment. Wing leaders suspected that some of the maintenance and logistics structures erected to support the F-15 were geared more to the environment and pace of the development and training cycle. They feared, therefore, that this situation might leave the wing unable to maintain planned sortie production rates away from its home station. The early deployment cycle "produced beneficial pressures to shift gears and the support system responded." During five deployments conducted from July to December

V - Back to TAC

1976 (four Red Flag's at Nellis and an E-3 Airborne Warning and Control System air defense test at McChord AFB, Washington), the deployed forces (eight F-15s at Nellis for each of the Red Flag's, twenty-four F-15s at McChord) maintained a sortie production rate of .978, or roughly one sortie per aircraft per day. The mission-capable rate achieved during these deployments averaged 74 percent. Both were credible figures for a brand-new, complex weapon system.[20]

The wing's next major structural change came in the spring of 1977, when the maintenance complex was reorganized under TAC's Production Oriented Maintenance Organization (POMO) concept. The command developed the POMO structure to ensure that its wings were organized and trained together in peacetime as they would deploy and fight together in war. To this end, the four-squadron maintenance structure was realigned to three squadrons. After a transitional phase from 1 April to 15 June 1977, HQ TAC formally established the new structure. The 1st Organizational Maintenance Squadron was redesignated the 1st Aircraft Generation Squadron (AGS), the 1st Field Maintenance Squadron became the 1st Equipment Maintenance Squadron (EMS), and the 1st Avionics Maintenance Squadron was redesignated the 1st Component Repair Squadron (CRS). The 1st Munitions Maintenance Squadron was inactivated; most of its functions were assumed by the 1st EMS. A further subdivision of the 1st AGS created the 27th, 71st, and 94th Aircraft Maintenance Units, flightline maintenance organizations aligned, as their names implied, with the flying squadron they supported. By 15 June 1977 the 1st Tactical Fighter Wing had assumed its contemporary structure.[21]

After successfully completing several deployments within the United States, the wing was ready to try its hand at more demanding foreign deployments. The 94th Tactical Fighter Squadron deployed eight aircraft to Korea, Japan, and the Phillipines from 21 January to 4 March 1978. The 94th and the 71st each deployed eighteen F-15s to the Netherlands from 13 September to 20 December 1978, with the 71st replacing the 94th on 27 October. Personnel from the 94th had barely unpacked their bags before they were off again, this time on a short-notice, sixteen-day, twelve-aircraft show-the-flag deployment to Saudi Arabia (Prized Eagle, 12-27 January 1979). The 27th deployed next, sending eight aircraft to Korea and Japan from 1-28 March 1979. Further deployments, to exercises within the continental United States, and to Europe, the Middle East, Southwest Asia, and the Pacific, have followed since then.[22]

Although the 1st TFW entered the 1980's full of optimism based on its performance since 1976, the early years of the decade proved a difficult time for the wing. On 7 June 1980 a HQ TAC Inspector General (IG) team kicked off an operational readiness inspection (ORI) of the 1st TFW. Five days later, on 12 June, a headline in the Hampton, Virginia, Daily Press reported that "Langley F-15 Jets Flunk Readiness Test." Wing officials refused to confirm or deny that interpretation of what transpired, but they did admit that the wing's spare parts situation had deteriorated. As a result, the mission-capable rate of the wing's F-15s had fallen to about forty percent. The wing's problems in 1980 paralleled those of TAC, the Air Force, and the nation's armed services as a whole. Spare parts were in short supply in many places. This grounded aircraft. Pilots who could not fly quickly became unhappy pilots. As morale dropped, retention rates fell too. The situation was not a happy one.[23]

The wing eventually overcame these trials. Improved funding provided more spare parts; this, plus a wide variety of other unit, command, and service initiatives, did much to improve wing morale. Retention rates stabilized, then climbed to peacetime highs. The TAC IG returned to the wing in August 1982. Results achieved this time reflected how the wing's personnel had turned the situation around. At a press conference on 19 August, Brigadier General Eugene H. Fischer, wing commander, reported that in four days of concentrated operations, wing aircraft had flown almost 1,100 sorties, or twenty-six percent more sorties than the inspection team asked the wing to fly. General Fischer expressed his pride in both the wing and the F-15, which, he noted, had suffered from an unfavorable reputation in the press for some time. He hoped that the wing's performance would dispel any lingering complaints that the aircraft was too complicated to be reliable. He added that the ORI had shown that the wing could perform as expected in a crisis. Wing leaders at all levels supported General Fischer's claim that the wing's performance in 1982 was the result of better planning and training, improved morale, and a greatly improved supply situation.[24]

The 65th anniversary of the organization of the 1st Pursuit Group, 5 May 1983, found the 1st Tactical Fighter Wing deployed to Phelps Collins Air National Guard Base, Alpena, Michigan. An area long familiar with the sound of the 1st Pursuit Group's fighters accustomed itself to the sixty F-15s that spent about five weeks in Michigan while contractors repaved the main runway at Langley.[25]

The 1982 ORI and events that followed served notice that the 1st Tactical Fighter Wing had completed the difficult climb back to peak capability. The wing completed a series of scheduled and unscheduled deployments that proved that the results achieved during the ORI were no fluke. The Air Force, too, noted that the wing was back. On 11 January 1985, it presented the wing with its second Air Force Outstanding Unit Award, which cited the wing for "exceptionally meritorious service from 15 June 1982 to 15 June 1984." The award noted the wing's "conspicuously outstanding performance" in a variety of operations that "contributed significantly to the international reputation of the United States and the Air Force as dynamic symbols of freedom throughout the world." The most telling acolade was the award's acknowledgement that the wing had "established the reputation... as the premier F-15 wing in Tactical Air Command." In 1970, the wing claimed for itself the title "First, as acknowledged." Fifteen years later, the Air Force acknowledged it too.[26]

V - Back to TAC

Photo V-1

McDonnell Douglas F-4 Phantom II,
1st Tactical Fighter Wing, MacDill AFB, Florida

Photo V-2

McDonnell Douglas F-15A, "Eagle Day"
Landing of the first F-15A, 9 January 1976

V - Back to TAC

Photo V-3

The flightline at Langley AFB during READY EAGLE.
The F-15s with the FF tail codes belong ot the 1st TFW.
Those with the BT tail codes belong to the 36th TFW, Bitburg AB, Germany.

Photo V-4
McDonnell Douglas TF-15A,
1st Tactical Fighter Wing, Langley AFB, Virginia,
20 March 1976

Appendices

Appendices

Appendix I, 1st Tactical Fighter Wing Lineage 87

Appendix II, Honors 89

II-1	Rickenbacker Congressional Medal of Honor	90
II-2	Luke Congressional Medal of Honor	91
II-3	Distinguished Unit Citation, 25 August 1943	92
II-4	Distinguished Unit Citation, 30 August 1943	93
II-5	Distinguished Unit Citation, 18 May 1944	94
II-6	Air Force Outstanding Unit Award, 1 March 1978	95
II-7	Air Force Outstanding Unit Award, 11 January 1985.	96

Appendix III, Organization 97

III-1	World War I	98
III-2	1919-1935	100
III-3	1935-1941	102
III-4	World War II	104
III-5	3 July 1946	106
III-6	15 August 1947	108
III-7	1948-1949	110
III-8	31 December 1950	112
III-9	6 February 1952	114
III-10	18 October 1956	116
III-11	1 February 1961	118
III-12	16 January 1967	120
III-13	1 October 1970	122
III-14	1 July 1971	124
III-15	19 April 1976	126
III-16	15 June 1977	128
III-17	5 May 1983	130

Appendix IV, Group and Wing Commanders 133

Appendix I

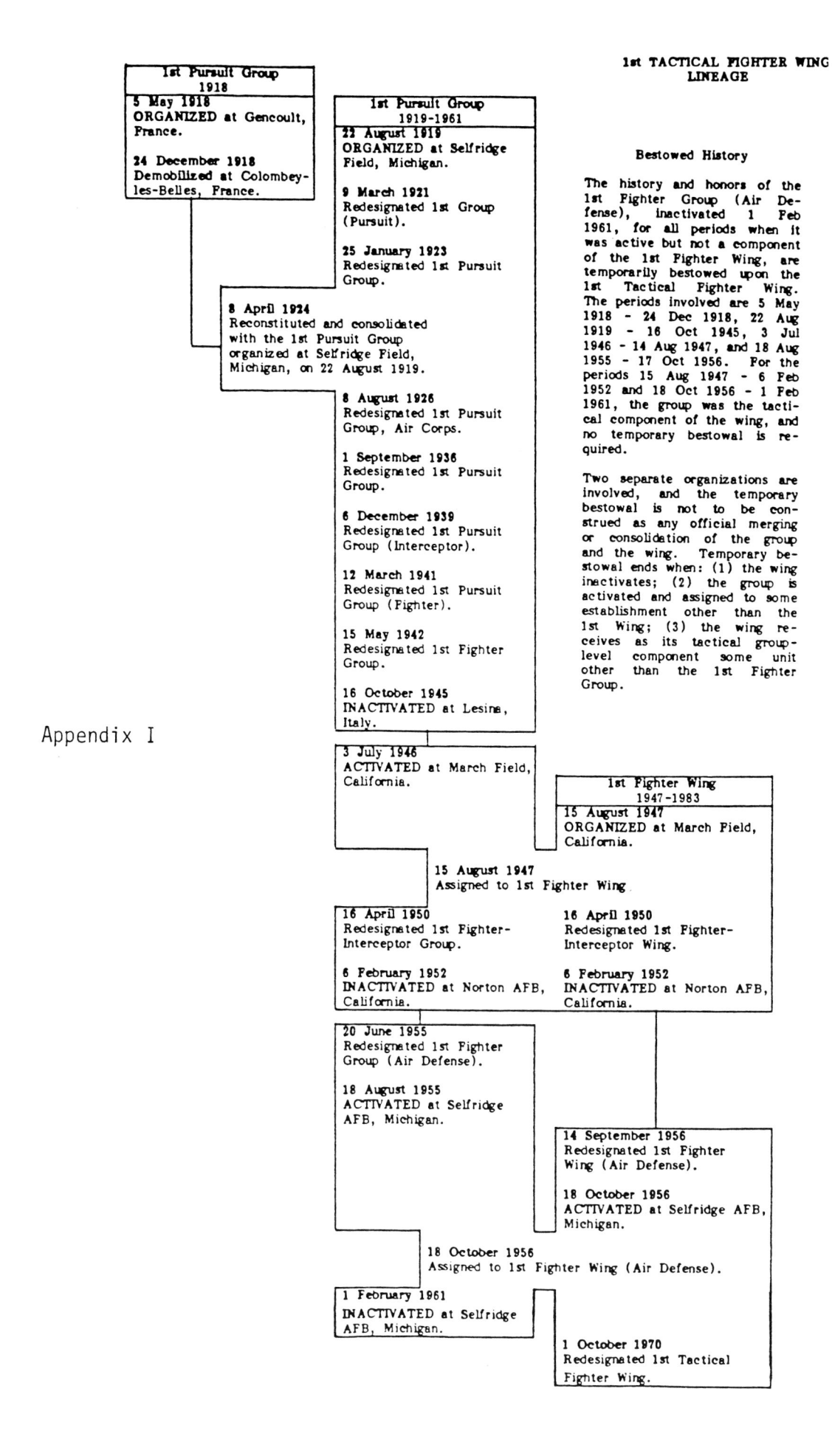

1st TACTICAL FIGHTER WING LINEAGE

1st Pursuit Group 1918

5 May 1918
ORGANIZED at Gengoult, France.

24 December 1918
Demobilized at Colombey-les-Belles, France.

1st Pursuit Group 1919-1961

22 August 1919
ORGANIZED at Selfridge Field, Michigan.

9 March 1921
Redesignated 1st Group (Pursuit).

25 January 1923
Redesignated 1st Pursuit Group.

8 April 1924
Reconstituted and consolidated with the 1st Pursuit Group organized at Selfridge Field, Michigan, on 22 August 1919.

8 August 1926
Redesignated 1st Pursuit Group, Air Corps.

1 September 1936
Redesignated 1st Pursuit Group.

6 December 1939
Redesignated 1st Pursuit Group (Interceptor).

12 March 1941
Redesignated 1st Pursuit Group (Fighter).

15 May 1942
Redesignated 1st Fighter Group.

16 October 1945
INACTIVATED at Lesina, Italy.

3 July 1946
ACTIVATED at March Field, California.

15 August 1947
Assigned to 1st Fighter Wing.

16 April 1950
Redesignated 1st Fighter-Interceptor Group.

6 February 1952
INACTIVATED at Norton AFB, California.

20 June 1955
Redesignated 1st Fighter Group (Air Defense).

18 August 1955
ACTIVATED at Selfridge AFB, Michigan.

18 October 1956
Assigned to 1st Fighter Wing (Air Defense).

1 February 1961
INACTIVATED at Selfridge AFB, Michigan.

1st Fighter Wing 1947-1983

15 August 1947
ORGANIZED at March Field, California.

16 April 1950
Redesignated 1st Fighter-Interceptor Wing.

6 February 1952
INACTIVATED at Norton AFB, California.

14 September 1956
Redesignated 1st Fighter Wing (Air Defense).

18 October 1956
ACTIVATED at Selfridge AFB, Michigan.

1 October 1970
Redesignated 1st Tactical Fighter Wing.

Bestowed History

The history and honors of the 1st Fighter Group (Air Defense), inactivated 1 Feb 1961, for all periods when it was active but not a component of the 1st Fighter Wing, are temporarily bestowed upon the 1st Tactical Fighter Wing. The periods involved are 5 May 1918 - 24 Dec 1918, 22 Aug 1919 - 16 Oct 1945, 3 Jul 1946 - 14 Aug 1947, and 18 Aug 1955 - 17 Oct 1956. For the periods 15 Aug 1947 - 6 Feb 1952 and 18 Oct 1956 - 1 Feb 1961, the group was the tactical component of the wing, and no temporary bestowal is required.

Two separate organizations are involved, and the temporary bestowal is not to be construed as any official merging or consolidation of the group and the wing. Temporary bestowal ends when: (1) the wing inactivates; (2) the group is activated and assigned to some establishment other than the 1st Wing; (3) the wing receives as its tactical group-level component some unit other than the 1st Fighter Group.

Appendix II - Honors

Appendix II

1st Tactical Fighter Wing

Honors

Distinguished Unit Citations

Italy, 25 August 1943
Italy, 30 August 1943
Rumania, 18 May 1944

Air Force Outstanding Unit Awards

1 July 1975 - 31 October 1976
15 June 1982 - 15 June 1984

Campaign Streamers

World War I

Champagne-Marne	Aisne-Marne
Oise-Aisne	St Mihel
Meuse-Argonne	Lorraine
Champagne	

World War II

Algeria-French Morocco	Tunisia
Sicily	Naples-Foggia
Anzio	Rome-Arno
Southern France	North Appenines
Po Valley	Air Offensive, Europe
Normandy	Northern France
Rhineland	Central Europe
Air Combat	

Bestowed History

The honors of the 1st Fighter Group, for all periods when it was active but not a component of the 1st Fighter Wing, are temporarily bestowed upon the 1st Tactical Fighter Wing. The periods involved are 5 May 1918 - 24 Dec 1918, 22 Aug 1919 - 16 Oct 1945, 3 Jul 1946 - 14 Aug 1947, and 18 Aug 1955 - 17 Oct 1956. For the periods 15 Aug 1947 - 6 Feb 1952 and 18 Oct 1956 - 1 Feb 1961, the group was the tactical component of the wing, and no temporary bestowal is required.

Citation to Accompany the Award of the

Congressional Medal of Honor

to

First Lieutenant Edward V. Rickenbacker
94th Aero Squadron

For Action near Billy, France,
on 25 September 1918

For conspicuous gallantry and intrepidity above and beyond the call of duty in action against the enemy near Billy, France, 25 September 1918. While on a voluntary patrol over the lines, Lieutenant Rickenbacker attacked seven enemy planes (five type Fokker, protecting two type Halberstadt). Disregarding the odds against him, he dived on them and shot down one of the Fokkers out of control. He then attacked one of the Halberstadts and sent it down also.

War Department
General Order 2, 1931

Appendix II-2

Citation to Accompany the Award of the

Congressional Medal of Honor

to

Second Lieutenant Frank Luke, Jr.
27th Aero Squadron

For Action Near Murvaux, France,
on 29 September 1918

After having previously destroyed a number of enemy aircraft within seventeen days, he voluntarily started on a patrol after German observation balloons. Though pursued by eight German planes which were protecting the enemy balloon line, he unhesitatingly attacked and shot down in flames three German balloons, being himself under heavy fire from ground batteries and hostile planes. Severely wounded, he descended to within fifty meters of the ground, and flying at this low altitude near the town of Murvaux, opened fire upon enemy troops, killing six and wounding as many more. Forced to make a landing, and surrounded on all sides by the enemy, who called upon him to surrender, he drew his automatic pistol and defended himself gallantly until he fell dead from a wound in the chest.

War Department
General Order 59, 1919

DISTINGUISHED UNIT CITATION

For action over Salerno, Italy,
on 25 August 1943

The **1st Fighter Group** is cited for outstanding performance of duty in armed conflict with the enemy. Upon receiving orders for the first mass long-range low-level strafing raid ever carried out, the pilots of the group spent three days intensely training and preparing for this vital operation, while ground personnel displayed the greatest zeal, devotion, and efficiency in preparing the P-38 type aircraft for this important mission. On 25 August 1943 sixty-five P-38's of the group took off to rendezvous with two other fighter groups for the attack on the Foggia airdromes, on which were concentrated more than 230 enemy aircraft which severely threatened the projected invasion at Salerno, Italy, and which, because of wide dispersal, were immune from normal bombing methods. In order to prevent detection by enemy radar it was imperative to fly the entire 530 miles to the target at an extremely low altitude. Serious losses were inevitable should the enemy be alerted. Completely disregarding antiaircraft fire, intense small arms fire, and possible enemy aerial opposition, the pilots by superb navigation swept across Italy and then northward where they split off for their respective attacks on the different Foggia airdromes. The heroic pilots of the **1st Fighter Group** swept across the enemy fields, strafing the widely dispersed aircraft, gun positions, enemy troops, and other military targets. In this attack the **1st Fighter Group** destroyed or severely damaged a total of eighty-eight hostile aircraft, with a loss of only two P-38's, while the entire mission accounted for a total of 150 aircraft destroyed or damaged on the ground. Thus, at this critical time before the landings at Salerno, a crippling blow was dealt to the enemy. The pilots of this group, despite all dangers, pressed their attacks with extraordinary heroism, covered both themselves and their group with glory, and rendered a valuable contribution to the armed conflict against our enemies in Europe, which is in keeping with the spirit and tradition of the armed forces of the United States.

War Department
General Order 66, 1944

Appendix II-4

DISTINGUISHED UNIT CITATION

For action over Aversa, Italy,
on 30 August 1943

The **1st Fighter Group** is cited for outstanding performance of duty against the enemy. On 30 August 1943, the **1st Fighter Group** was assigned the vital mission as escort to two medium bombardment groups which were attacking the important marshalling yards at Aversa, Italy. Crossing the Italian coast, their formation of forty-four aircraft was intercepted by approximately seventy-five highly aggressive and persistent enemy fighter aircraft. Alone and unaided, the **1st Fighter Group** gallantly engaged this formidable hostile force, beating off wave after wave of enemy airplanes attempting to pierce the fighter defenses to attack and break up the bomber formation. Despite the overwhelming superiority in numbers of enemy fighters, demonstrating the greatest skill in escort duty, with superior flying skill, determination, and aggressiveness, these courageous pilots fought a brilliant defensive aerial battle, destroying eight, probably destroying three, and damaging three enemy fighter aircraft, while our own losses totaled thirteen missing. Through their highly effective fighter cover, the bomber formation was enabled to complete a highly successful bombing run unmolested, inflicting grave damage to vital installations, and return to base without the loss of a single bomber. By the superior technical skill and devotion to duty exhibited by the ground personnel, whose tireless efforts made this vital mission possible, together with the conspicuous courage, fortitude, and aggressive combat spirit of the pilots, the **1st Fighter Group** upheld the highest traditions of the military service, thereby reflecting great credit on themselves and the armed forces of the United States.

War Department
General Order 44, 1946

DISTINGUISHED UNIT CITATION

For action over Ploesti, Rumania
on 18 May 1944

The **1st Fighter Group** is cited for outstanding performance of duty in armed conflict with the enemy. On 18 May 1944, 146 B-17s of the Fifteenth Air Force were dispatched to attack the Ploesti Romano Americano Oil Refinery in Rumania, a very important and heavily defended element in the enemy oil production complex. P-38's of the **1st Fighter Group** were assigned the task of covering the withdrawal of the bomber forces. En route such bad weather was encountered that the fighter group would have been justified in returning to base. However, they elected to continue on course on the chance that some of the bombers had been able to get through and needed withdrawal cover. Expert navigation in aircraft not equipped for dead reckoning, skillful formation discipline, and the admirable state of plane repair and maintenance enabled the P-38's to reach the rendezvous area after a hazardous trip of 450 miles over enemy territory. There they found that only one group of bombers, instead of four as planned, had been able to get through the weather to the target, and this one group was found to be under vicious attack by some eighty enemy fighters, having already lost six bombers in the battle. Although badly outnumbered, and their efforts complicated by severe and adverse weather conditions, the pilots of the **1st Fighter Group** heroically took over the defense of the returning bombers, pressing the attack so skillfully and courageously that the bomber force was able to proceed to base without additional loss. The fighters continued to battle the enemy until all had been driven off and in aerial combat destroyed ten enemy planes, probably destroyed three, and damaged six, with one P-38 lost, the pilot successfully parachuting to safety en route to base. The unwavering determination of this group to accomplish their mission despite the weather, the top mechanical condition of their planes, and above all the bravery and skill of these badly outnumbered pilots, enabled the **1st Fighter Group** to save the bombers from further loss. The victory so achieved over a superior force was a fitting climax to the heavy damage inflicted on the target by the B-17's and demonstrates the greatest devotion to duty on the part of all who were responsible for the condition of the P-38's, the staff planning attending the operation, the degree of training reflected in its brilliant execution, and the bravery and efficiency of those who finally executed it. Such accomplishments evidence the finest traditions of the military service and reflect great credit on the **1st Fighter Group** and the armed forces of the United States of America.

War Department
General Order 75, 1944

Appendix II-6

Citation to Accompany the Award of the

Air Force Outstanding Unit Award

to the

1st Tactical Fighter Wing

The 1st Tactical Fighter Wing, Tactical Air Command, distinguished itself by exceptionally meritorious service from 1 July 1974 to 31 October 1976. During this period, personnel and units of the 1st Tactical Fighter Wing introduced the F-15 weapon system into the operational inventory and brought it to its initial combat ready status. They provided continuous airborne command post capability for the Commander in Chief, Atlantic Command, and maintained administrative support aircraft for Headquarters, Tactical Air Command. The professionalism and dedication to duty demonstrated by the members of the 1st Tactical Fighter Wing reflect great credit on themselves and the United States Air Force.

>Department of the Air Force
>Special Order GB-116
>1 March 1978

Citation to Accompany the Award of the

Air Force Outstanding Unit Award

to the

1st Tactical Fighter Wing

The 1st Tactical Fighter Wing, Tactical Air Command, Langley Air Force Base, Virginia, distinguished itself by exceptionally meritorious service from 15 June 1982 to 15 June 1984. The wing's conspicuously outstanding performance while engaged in its primary role as lead F-15 unit supporting Central Command contributed significantly to the international reputation of the United States and the Air Force as dynamic symbols of freedom throughout the world. Continuously superior performances in national and international exercises established the reputation of this unit as the premier F-15 wing in Tactical Air Command reflecting superior expertise in the air-to-air combat arena. The dynamic and timely response to real world contingency requirements amply illustrated the outstanding mobility capabilities and combat potential of the wing and the resolve of the United States to overtly support its foreign policy objectives from the Caribbean to Southwest Asia. The outstanding Major Air Command inspection results sustained by the 1st Tactical Fighter Wing and the numerous unit and individual awards it has received are further substantial evidence of the unsurpassed dedication and professionalism of the men and women of this unit. The professionalism and dedication to duty demonstrated by members of the 1st Tactical Fighter Wing reflect credit upon themselves and the United States Air Force.

Department of the Air Force
Special Order GB-004
11 January 1985

Appendix III

Organization

III-1	5 May 1918 - 24 December 1918	98
III-2	1919-1934	100
III-3	1935-1941	102
III-4	World War II	104
III-5	3 July 1946	106
III-6	15 August 1947	108
III-7	1948-1949	110
III-8	31 December 1950	112
III-9	6 February 1952	114
III-10	18 October 1956	116
III-11	1 February 1961	118
III-12	16 January 1967	120
III-13	1 October 1970	122
III-14	1 July 1971	124
III-15	19 April 1976	126
III-16	15 June 1977	128
III-17	5 May 1983	130

Appendix III-1

Organization, 1st Pursuit Group
5 May 1918 - 24 December 1918

The AEF assigned the 94th and 95th Aero Squadrons to the 1st Pursuit Group on 5 May 1918, the 27th and 147th on 31 May, the 218th Aero Construction Squadron on 6 August, the 4th Air Park on 24 August, and the 185th Aero Squadron on 7 October. The 94th Aero Squadron was relieved from assignment to the 1st Pursuit Group on 17 November 1918 and assigned to the Third Army. The 4th Air Park was relieved from assignment to the group on 18 November 1918.

Abbreviations

AS	Aero Squadron	AP	Air Park
ACS	Aero Construction Squadron		

Appendix III-1

Organization, 1st Pursuit Group
5 May - 24 December 1918

5 May - 6 August 1918

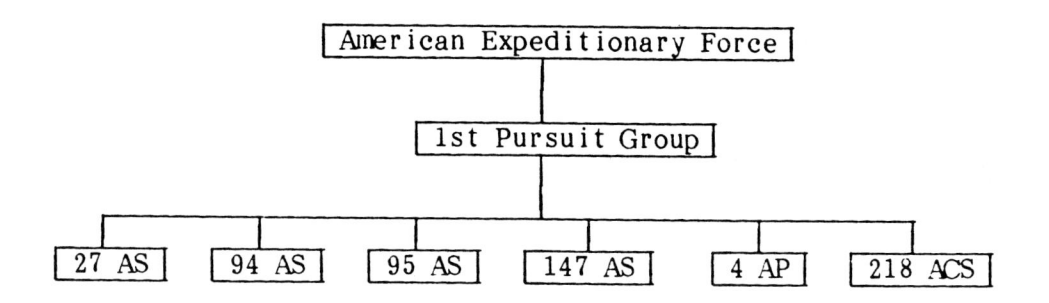

```
American Expeditionary Force
            |
     1st Pursuit Group
            |
 ┌──────┬──────┬──────┬──────┬──────┐
27 AS  94 AS  95 AS  147 AS  4 AP  218 ACS
```

30 August - 24 December 1918

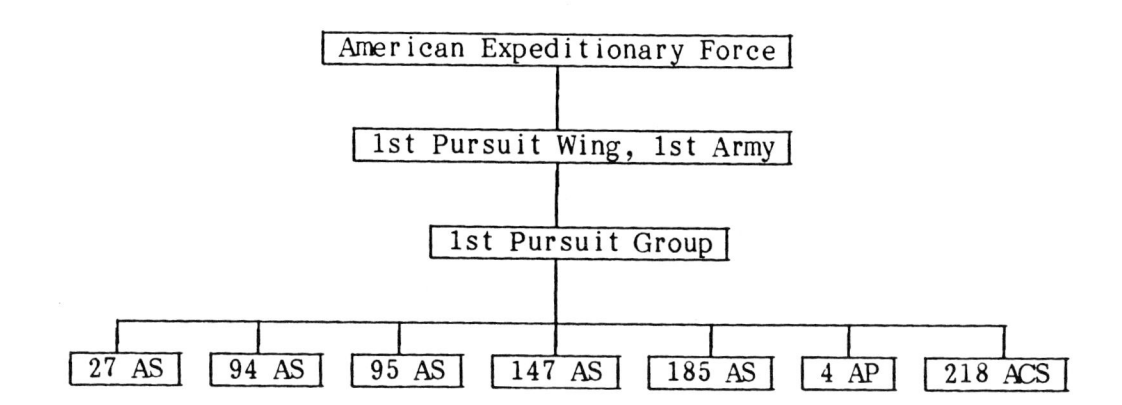

```
American Expeditionary Force
            |
  1st Pursuit Wing, 1st Army
            |
     1st Pursuit Group
            |
 ┌──────┬──────┬──────┬──────┬──────┬──────┐
27 AS  94 AS  95 AS  147 AS  185 AS  4 AP  218 ACS
```

Appendix III-2

Organization
1919 - 1934

Information concerning the group's assignments during this period is not available. In addition, the group's designation changed several times throughout the period. Consult Appendix 1, page 87, for information on the unit's designation as of a given date.

This chart reflects the group's organization from its activation at Selfridge Field, Michigan, 22 August 1919 through its stay at Kelly Field, Texas.

The War Department redesignated the 147th Pursuit Squadron the 17th Pursuit Squadron on 3 March 1921. It activated the 57th Services Squadron and assigned it to the 1st Pursuit Group on 27 June 1921. The group retained this organization when it returned to Selfridge in June 1922.

The War Department inactivated the 95th Pursuit Squadron on 31 July 1927. It attached the 36th Pursuit Squadron to the 1st Pursuit Group from 2 October 1930 to June 1932.

Abbreviations

| PS | Pursuit Squadron | SS | Services Squadron |

Appendix III-2

Organization
1919-1934

1919-1921

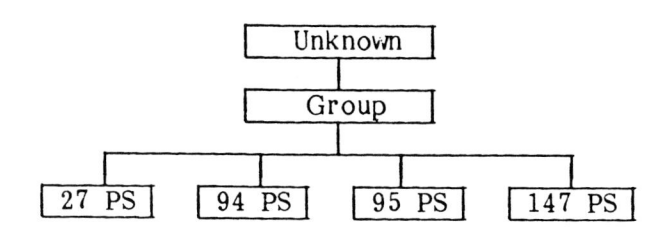

```
         Unknown
            |
          Group
   _____|_____
   |     |     |     |
 27 PS  94 PS  95 PS  147 PS
```

1921-1927

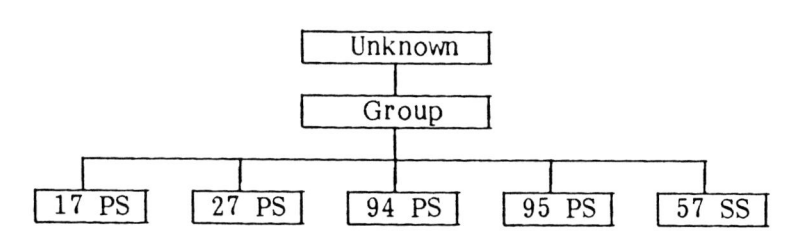

```
         Unknown
            |
          Group
  _____|_____
  |     |     |     |     |
17 PS  27 PS  94 PS  95 PS  57 SS
```

1927-1934

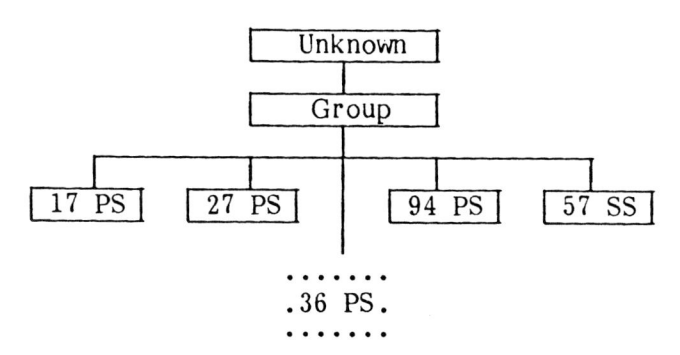

```
         Unknown
            |
          Group
  _____|_____
  |     |     |     |
17 PS  27 PS  94 PS  57 SS
            |
         .......
         .36 PS.
         .......
```

Appendix III-3

Organization
1935 - 1941

On 1 March 1935 the War Department activated General Headquarters, Air Force (GHQAF) at Langley Field, Virginia. It also activated the 2nd Wing, GHQAF, and assigned the 1st Pursuit Group to the wing. The War Department also activated the 56th Services Squadron, assigned it and the 57th Services Squadron to the 2d Wing, and attached both squadrons to the 1st Pursuit Group at Selfridge. Eighteen months later, on 1 September 1936, the War Department inactivated the two services squadrons, consolidated them, and redesignated the consolidated unit Headquarters and Headquarters Squadron, 1st Pursuit Group.

On 23 October 1940 the War Department relieved the 17th Pursuit Squadron from its assignment to the 1st Pursuit Group.

On 1 January 1941 the War Department activated the 71st Pursuit Squadron and assigned it to the 1st Pursuit Group at Selfridge Field, Michigan.

Abbreviations

PG	Pursuit Group	PS	Pursuit Squadron
SS	Services Squadron	Wg	Wing
GHQAF	General Headquarters, Air Force		

Appendix III-3

Organization
1935-1941

1935-1940

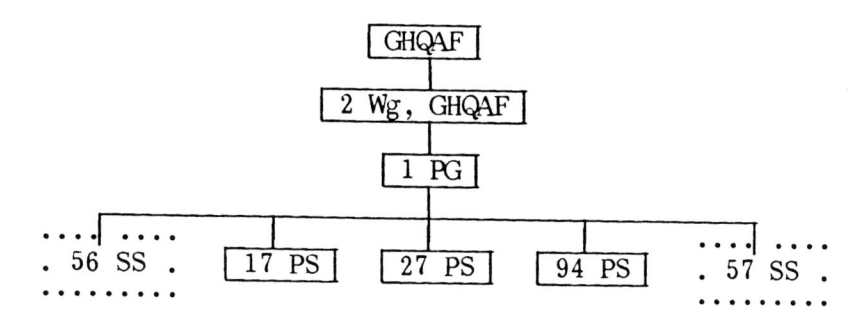

```
                    [GHQAF]
                       |
                 [2 Wg, GHQAF]
                       |
                    [1 PG]
    _____|_____
   |         |        |        |         |
 :56 SS:  [17 PS]  [27 PS]  [94 PS]  :57 SS:
```

October 1940

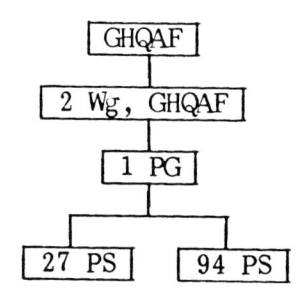

```
        [GHQAF]
           |
     [2 Wg, GHQAF]
           |
        [1 PG]
       ____|____
      |         |
   [27 PS]  [94 PS]
```

1 January 1941

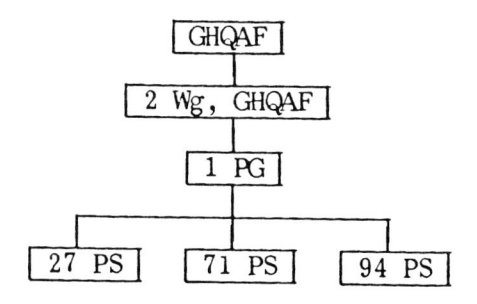

```
         [GHQAF]
            |
      [2 Wg, GHQAF]
            |
         [1 PG]
      _____|_____
     |      |      |
  [27 PS][71 PS][94 PS]
```

Appendix III-4

Organization
World War II

The organization of the 1st Fighter Group (a redesignation effective 15 May 1942) remained stable throughout the war, except for the assignment of the 1st Interceptor Control Squadron during the group's brief stay on the West Coast during the early days of the war.

Abbreviations

AF	Air Force
Bmbr	Bomber
BW	Bomb Wing
Cmbt	Combat
Cmd	Command
FG	Fighter Group
FS	Fighter Squadron
Ftr	Fighter
FW	Fighter Wing
GHQAF	General Headquarters Air Force
ICS	Interceptor Control Squadron
Intcptr	Interceptor
NEAD	Northeast Air District
NWAAF	Northwest African Air Forces
NWASAF	Northwest African Strategic Air Force
Prov	Provisional
PW	Pursuit Wing

Appendix III-4

Organization
World War II

15 Jan 42 - 13 May 42

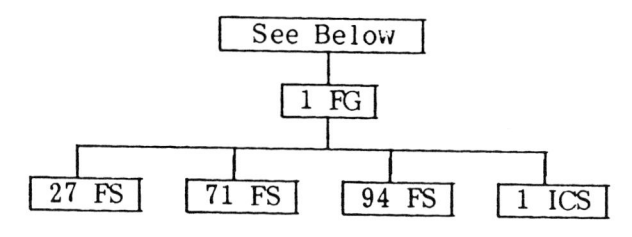

```
        ┌──────────┐
        │See Below │
        └────┬─────┘
          ┌──┴──┐
          │ 1 FG│
          └──┬──┘
    ┌────┬───┴───┬─────┐
  ┌─┴──┐┌─┴──┐┌──┴─┐┌──┴──┐
  │27 FS││71 FS││94 FS││1 ICS│
  └────┘└────┘└────┘└─────┘
```

13 May 42 - 16 Oct 45

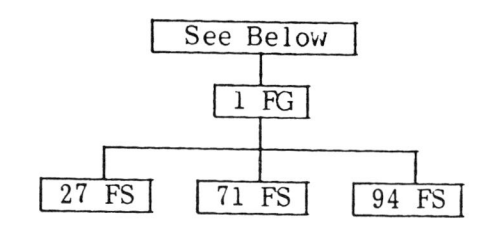

```
        ┌──────────┐
        │See Below │
        └────┬─────┘
          ┌──┴──┐
          │ 1 FG│
          └──┬──┘
      ┌─────┼─────┐
   ┌──┴─┐┌──┴─┐┌──┴─┐
   │27 FS││71 FS││94 FS│
   └────┘└────┘└────┘
```

Higher Headquarters
January 1941 - October 1945

```
16 Jan 41: GHQAF, NEAD, 6 PW
 9 Apr 41: GHQAF, 1 AF, I Inteptr Cmd, 6 PW
 5 Sep 41: AF Cmbt Cmd, 1 AF, I Bmbr Cmd
 9 Dec 41: AF Cmbt Cmd, 4 AF
   Jan 42: AF Cmbt Cmd, 4 AF, IV Inteptr Cmd
10 Jun 42: 8 AF, VIII Ftr Cmd
16 Aug 42: 8 AF, VIII Ftr Cmd, 6 FW
14 Sep 42: 12 AF, XII Ftr Cmd
24 Dec 42: 12 AF, XII Bmbr Cmd
18 Feb 43: NWAAF, NWASAF, 7 FW
   May 43: NWAAF, NWASAF, 5 BW
25 Jun 43: NWAAF, NWASAF, 2686 MBW (Prov)
24 Aug 43: NWAAF, NWASAF, 42 BW
 1 Sep 43: 12 AF, XII Bmbr Cmd
 1 Nov 43: 15 AF, 42 BW
   Jan 44: 15 AF, 5 BW
27 Mar 44: 15 AF, 306 BW
   Sep 44: 15 AF, XV Ftr Cmd (Prov), 305 FW (Prov)
   Jun 45: 15 AF, 305 BW
15 Sep 45: 305 BW
```

Appendix III-5

Organization
3 July 1946

The 1st Fighter Group activated on 3 July 1946 at March Field (later Air Force Base), California, was assigned to Tactical Air Command and Twelfth Air Force and equipped with P-80's (later F-80's).

Abbreviations

AF	Air Force
FG	Fighter Group
FS, J	Fighter Squadron, Jet
TAC	Tactical Air Command

Appendix III-5

Organization
3 July 1946

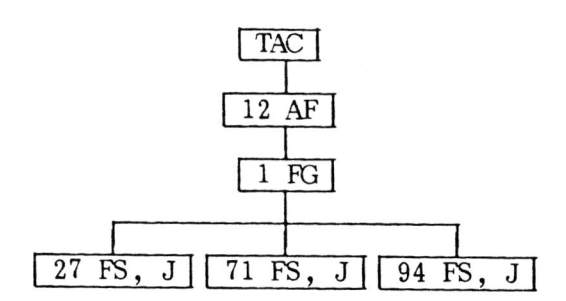

```
        ┌─────┐
        │ TAC │
        └──┬──┘
        ┌──┴───┐
        │ 12 AF│
        └──┬───┘
        ┌──┴──┐
        │ 1 FG│
        └──┬──┘
    ┌──────┼──────┐
┌───┴───┐┌─┴─────┐┌┴──────┐
│27 FS,J││71 FS,J││94 FS,J│
└───────┘└───────┘└───────┘
```

Appendix III-6

Organization
15 August 1947

The 1st Fighter Group and its three assigned squadrons became the tactical component of the 1st Fighter Wing when the wing activated on 15 August 1947 at March Field, California. The 67th Reconnaissance Group was also briefly assigned to the 1st Fighter Wing (15 August - 25 November 1947).

The six squadrons of the 1st Airdrome Group provided various services: Squadron A: communications; Squadron B, security; Squadron C, civil engineering; Squadron D, food services; Squadron E, transportation, and Squadron F, base services.

Appendix III-6

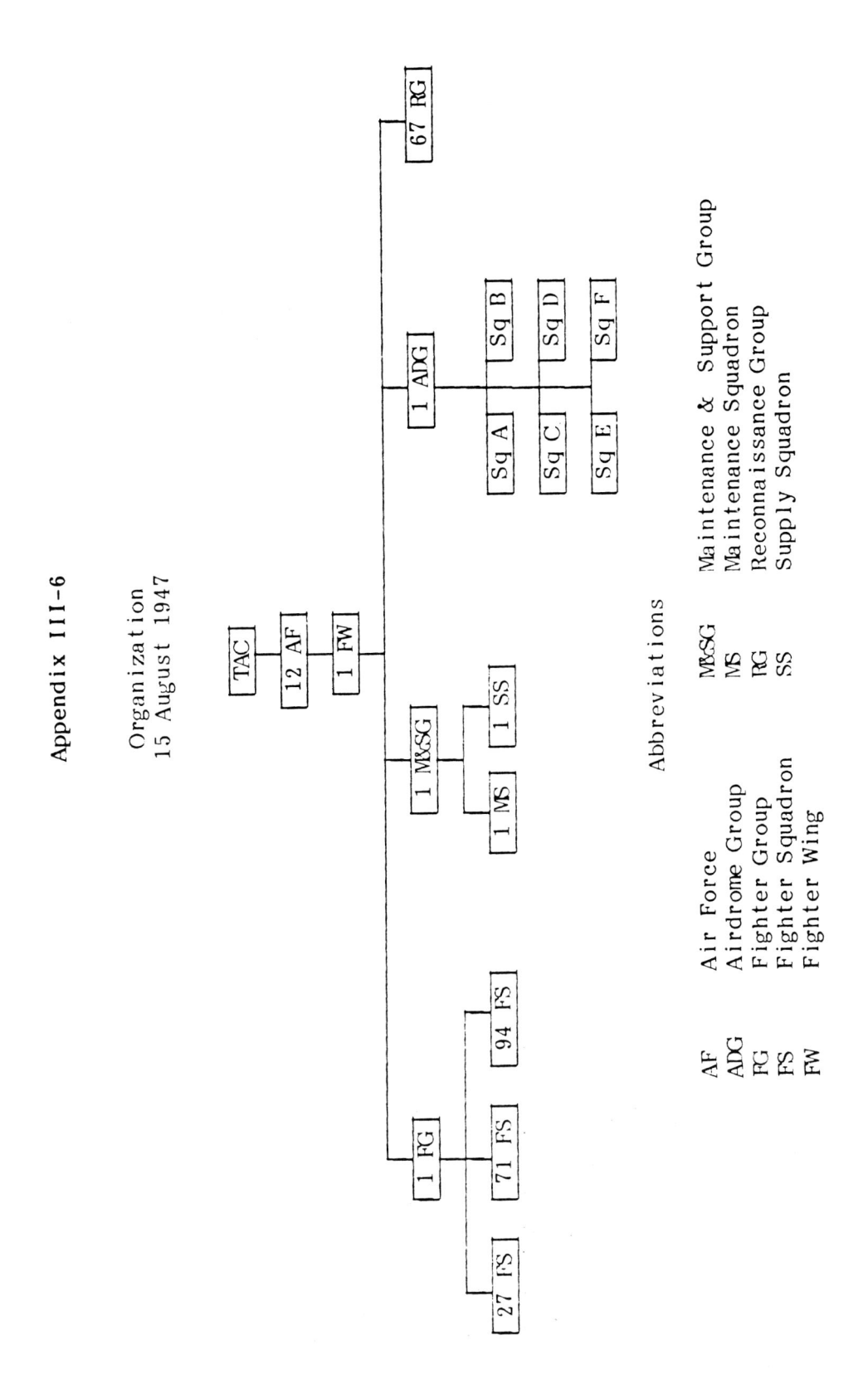

Organization
15 August 1947

```
                              TAC
                               |
                             12 AF
                               |
                             1 FW
                               |
        ┌──────────────────────┼──────────────────────┐
       1 FG                 1 M&SG                  1 ADG                67 RG
        │                     │                      │
   ┌────┼────┐            ┌───┴───┐         ┌────┬───┼───┬────┐
 27 FS 71 FS 94 FS      1 MS   1 SS       Sq A Sq B Sq C Sq D Sq E Sq F
```

Abbreviations

AF	Air Force	M&SG	Maintenance & Support Group
ADG	Airdrome Group	MS	Maintenance Squadron
FG	Fighter Group	RG	Reconnaissance Group
FS	Fighter Squadron	SS	Supply Squadron
FW	Fighter Wing		

Appendix III-7

Organization
1948 - 1949

While the wing's organization remained basically stable throughout this period, in less than two years it found itself assigned to three different major commands.

Abbreviations

AF	Air Force
ConAC	Continental Air Command
FW	Fighter Wing
SAC	Strategic Air Command
TAC	Tactical Air Command

Appendix III-7

Organization
1948 - 1949

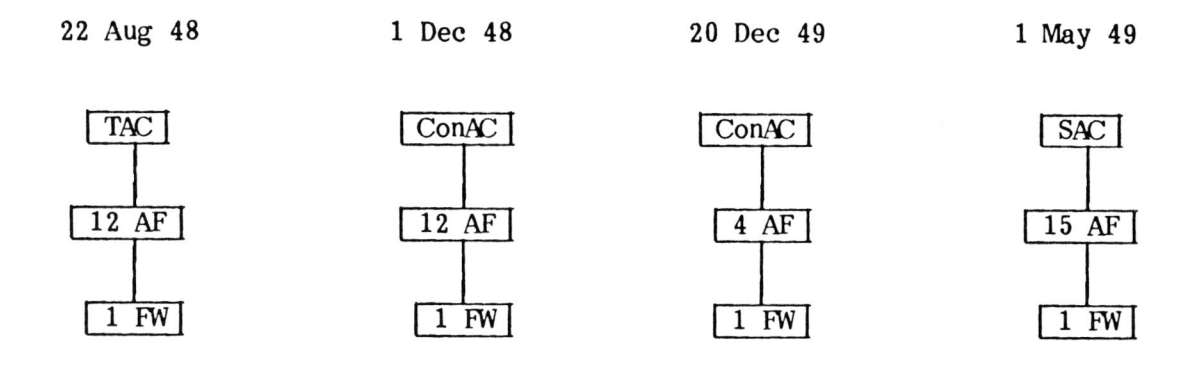

22 Aug 48	1 Dec 48	20 Dec 49	1 May 49
TAC	ConAC	ConAC	SAC
12 AF	12 AF	4 AF	15 AF
1 FW	1 FW	1 FW	1 FW

Appendix III-8

Organization
31 December 1950

The first chart shows the organization of the 1st Fighter-Interceptor Wing and its operational component, the 1st Fighter-Interceptor Group, as of 31 December 1950. The other two charts reflect the wing's actual placement in the ConAC system. The group and the two squadrons in the east remained assigned to the wing, but their placement left them outside its effective control. Their attachment to the EADF closed this gap in the chain of command.

Abbreviations

AF	Air Force
AFB	Air Force Base
ConAC	Continental Air Command
EADF	Eastern Air Defense Force
FIG	Fighter-Interceptor Group
FIS	Fighter-Interceptor Squadron
FIW	Fighter-Interceptor Wing
WADF	Western Air Defense Force

Appendix III-8

Appendix III-8

Organization
31 December 1950

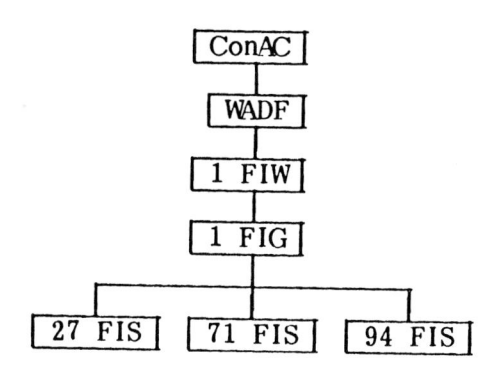

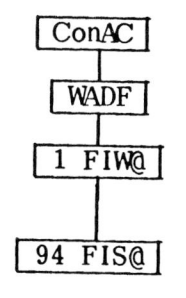

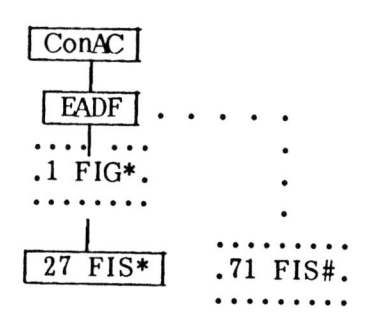

```
        ConAC
          |
         WADF
          |
         1 FIW
          |
         1 FIG
      ____|____
     |    |    |
  27 FIS 71 FIS 94 FIS
```

```
   ConAC              ConAC
     |                  |
   WADF               EADF . . . . . .
     |               ... | ...        .
   1 FIW@           . 1 FIG* .        .
     |              . . . . . . .     .
   94 FIS@                |       . . . . . . .
                       27 FIS*    . 71 FIS# .
                                  . . . . . . .
```

@ Stationed at George AFB, CA   * Stationed at Griffiss AFB, NY
                                    # Stationed at Pittsburgh Airport, PA

Appendix III-9

Organization
6 February 1952

On 6 February 1952, Air Defense Command inactivated the 1st Fighter-Interceptor Wing and the 1st Fighter-Interceptor Group and assigned the group's squadrons to newly organized "air defense wings."

Abbreviations

ADC	Air Defense Command
ADW	Air Defense Wing
EADF	Eastern Air Defense Force
WADF	Western Air Defense Force

Appendix III-9

Organization
6 February 1952

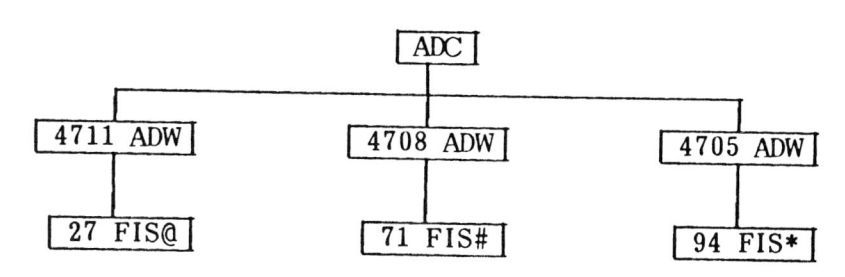

```
                    ┌─────┐
                    │ ADC │
                    └──┬──┘
         ┌─────────────┼─────────────┐
    ┌────┴────┐   ┌────┴────┐   ┌────┴────┐
    │4711 ADW │   │4708 ADW │   │4705 ADW │
    └────┬────┘   └────┬────┘   └────┬────┘
    ┌────┴────┐   ┌────┴────┐   ┌────┴────┐
    │ 27 FIS@ │   │ 71 FIS# │   │ 94 FIS* │
    └─────────┘   └─────────┘   └─────────┘
```

@ Stationed at Griffiss AFB, NY
\# Stationed at Pittsburgh Airport, PA
* Stationed at George AFB, CA

Appendix III-10

Organization
18 October 1956

This chart reflects the organization of the 1st Fighter Wing (Air Defense) as of its activation at Selfridge AFB, Michigan, on 18 October 1956. The 27 FIS was not assigned to the wing; it remained at Griffiss AFB.

Abbreviations

ABG	Air Base Group
AD	Air Defense
ADC	Air Defense Command
AD (D)	Air Division (Defense)
ADW	Air Defense Wing
APS	Air Police Squadron
DADS	Detroit Air Defense Sector
FG (AD)	Fighter Group (Air Defense)
FIS	Fighter-Interceptor Squadron
FMS	Field Maintenance Squadron
FSS	Food Services Squadron
FW (AD)	Fighter Wing (Air Defense)
IS	Installations Squadron
M&SG	Maintenance & Supply Group
OS	Operations Squadron
SS	Supply Squadron
TS	Transportation Squadron
WAFSS	Women's Air Force Squadron Section
USAFH	USAF Hospital

Appendix III-10

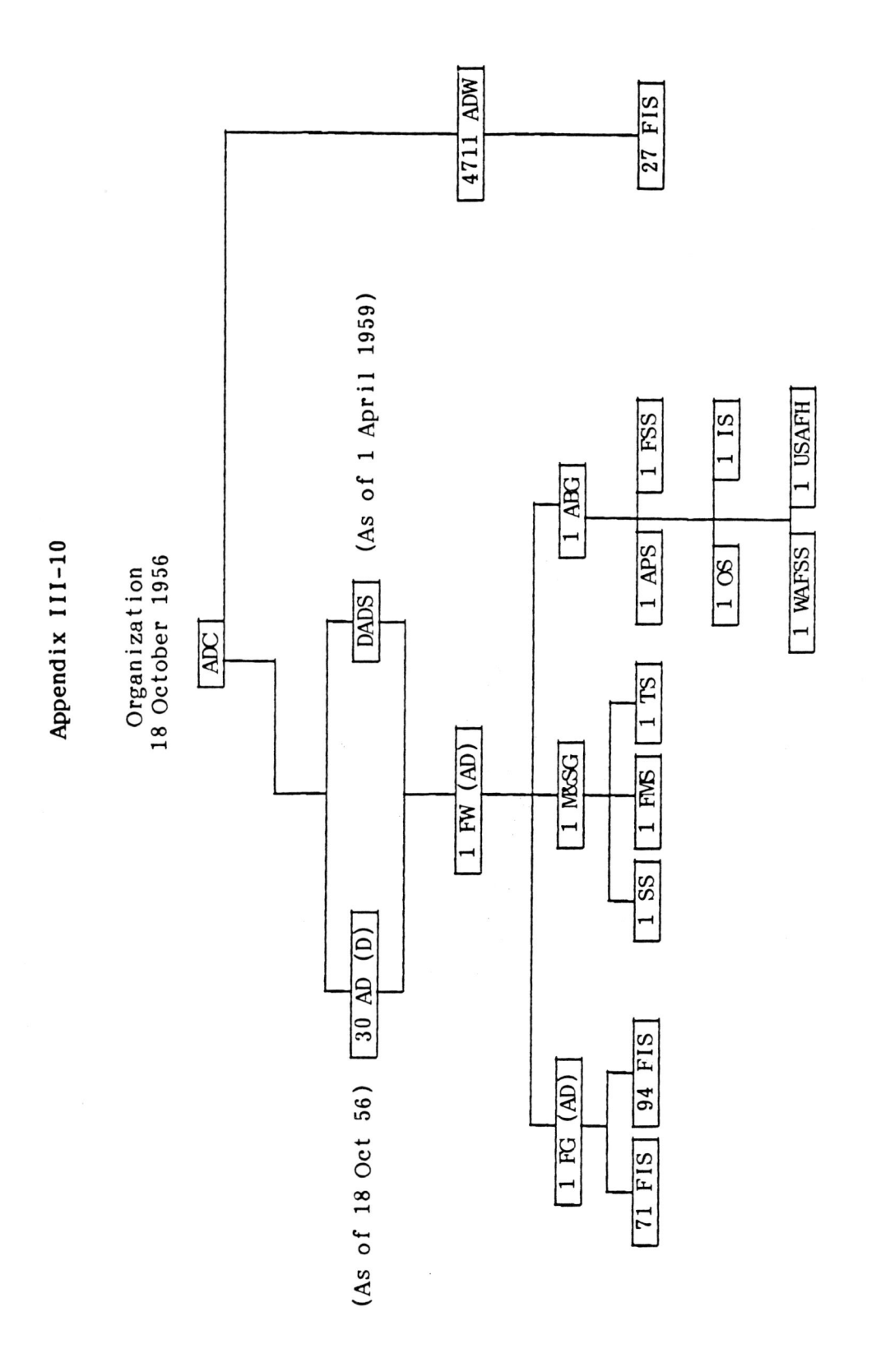

**Organization
18 October 1956**

```
                              ADC
                               |
        ┌──────────────────────┴──────────────────────┐
        |                                          4711 ADW
       DADS                                            |
  (As of 1 April 1959)                              27 FIS
        |
  ┌─────┴─────┐
30 AD (D)   1 FW (AD)
(As of 18 Oct 56)  |
        ┌──────────┼──────────┐
     1 FG (AD)  1 M&SG      1 ABG
        |         |           |
    ┌───┴───┐  ┌──┼──┐    ┌───┴───┐
  71 FIS 94 FIS 1 SS 1 FMS 1 TS  1 APS  1 FSS
                              1 OS   1 IS
                              1 WAFSS 1 USAFH
```

Appendix III-11

Organization
1 February 1961

Air Defense Command inactivated Headquarters, 1st Fighter Group (Air Defense) on 1 February 1961. A newly created Deputy Commander for Operations staff assumed its functions. Likewise, a new Deputy Commander for Maintenance staff assumed supervisory responsibility for maintenance functions. The 1st Fighter Wing (Air Defense) remained at Selfridge AFB, Michigan, at this time. The 27th Fighter-Interceptor Squadron continued to operate on the East Coast.

Abbreviations

ABG	Air Base Group
AD	Air Defense
ADC	Air Defense Command
A&ES	Armament & Electronics Squadron
APS	Air Police Squadron
BADS	Bangor Air Defense Sector
CES	Civil Engineering Squadron
CSS	Combat Support Squadron
DADS	Detroit Air Defense Sector
DC	Deputy Commander
FIS	Fighter-Interceptor Squadron
FMS	Field Maintenance Squadron
FW (AD)	Fighter Wing (Air Defense)
Maint	Maintenance
OMS	Organizational Maintenance Squadron
Ops	Operations
SS	Supply Squadron
TS	Transportation Squadron

Appendix III-11

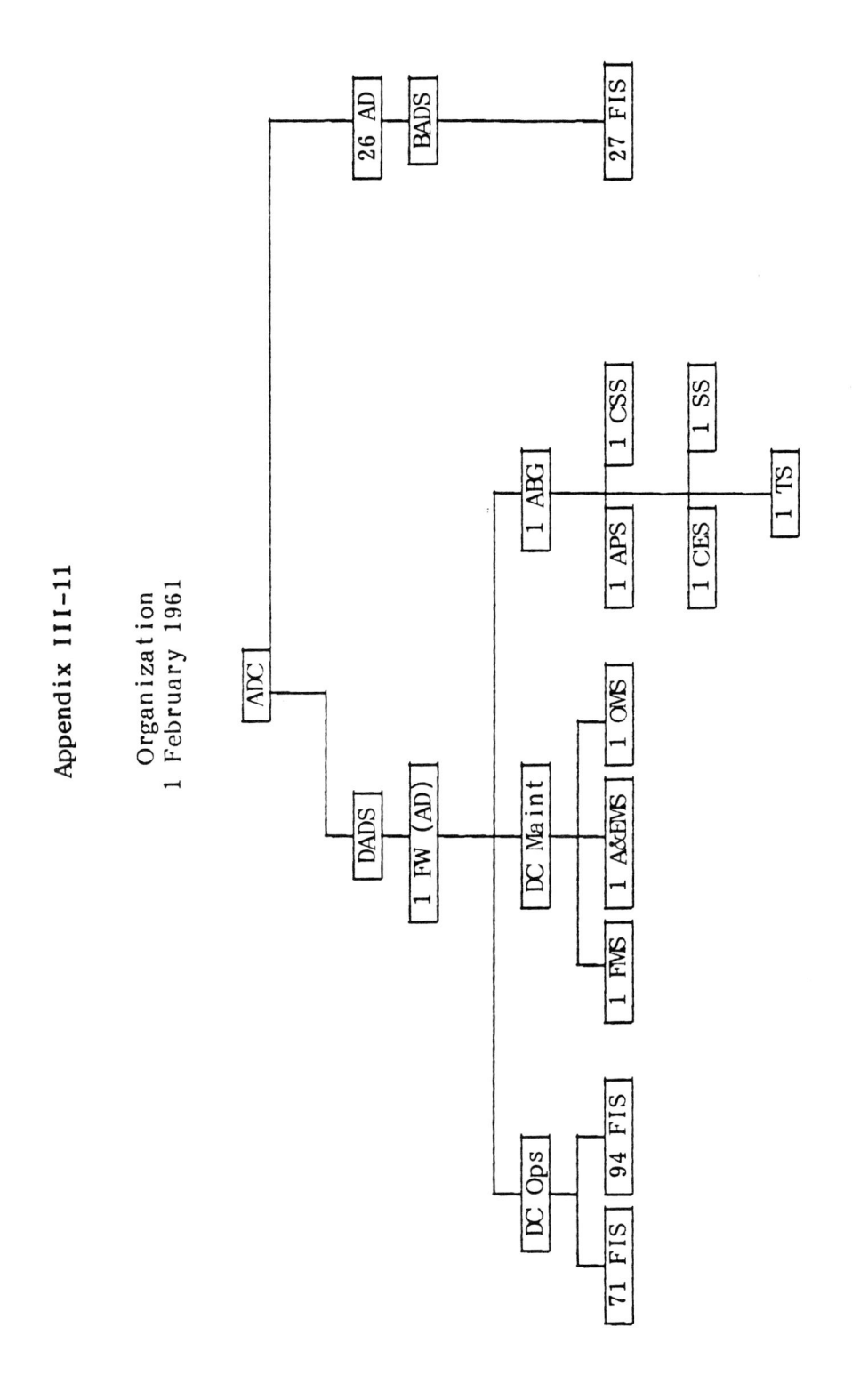

Organization
1 February 1961

```
                                    ADC
                                     |
            ┌────────────────────────┴─────────┐
            |                                  |
          DADS                               26 AD
            |                                BADS
         1 FW (AD)                             |
            |                                27 FIS
   ┌────────┼────────┬──────────┐
  DC Ops          DC Maint    1 ABG
   |               |            |
┌──┴──┐       ┌────┼────┐    ┌──┼────┐
71 FIS 94 FIS 1 FMS 1 A&EMS 1 OMS  1 APS  1 CSS
                                   1 CES  1 SS
                                   1 TS
```

Appendix III-12

Organization
16 January 1967

A series of organizational changes in the mid-1960's drastically altered the wing's organization. This chart shows the results of these changes and reflects the organization in effect in mid-January 1967.

Abbreviations

ADC	Air Defense Command
AD	Air Division
APS	Air Police Squadron
CES	Civil Engineering Squadron
CMS	Consolidated Maintenance Squadron
CSG	Combat Support Group
DC	Deputy Commander
FIS	Fighter-Interceptor Squadron
FSS	Food Services Squadron
FW (AD)	Fighter Wing (Air Defense)
HQ Sq Sect	Headquarters Squadron Section
Mat	Materiel
Ops	Operations
SS	Supply Squadron
TS	Transportation Squadron
WAFS	Women's Air Force Squadron

Appendix III-12

Organization
16 January 1967

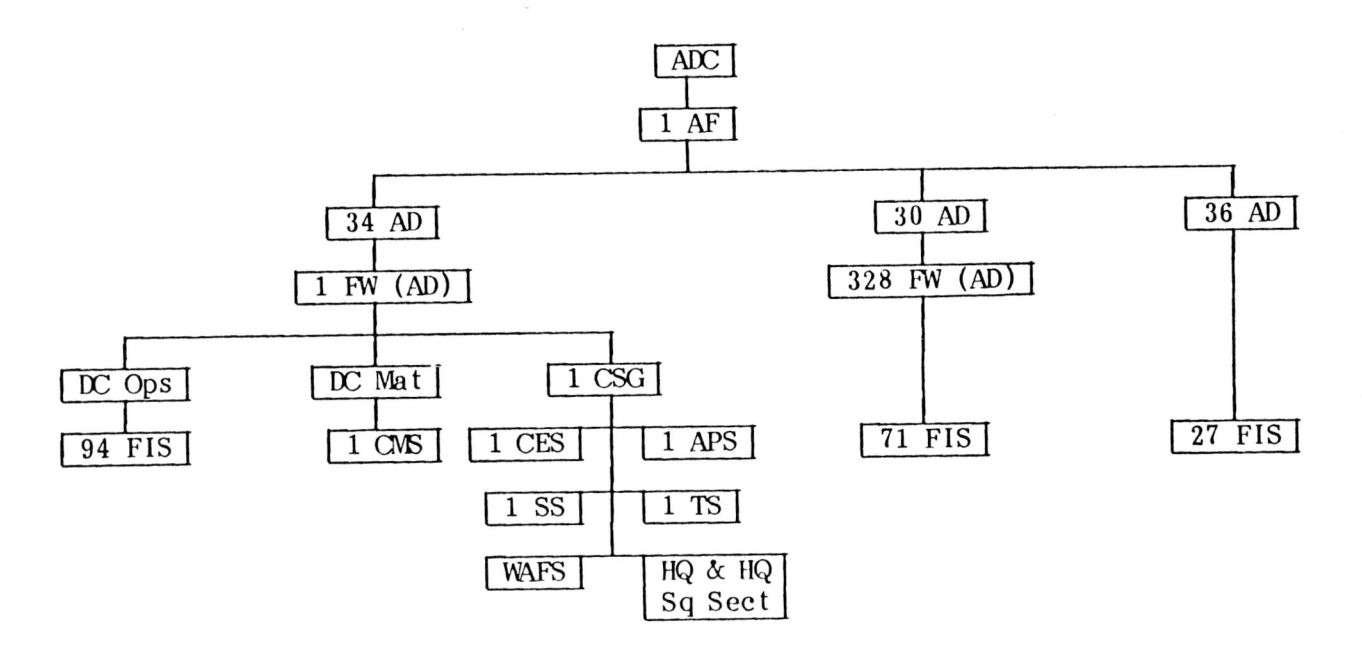

```
                          ADC
                           |
                          1 AF
        _____|_____
       |                   |                   |
      34 AD               30 AD              36 AD
       |                   |                   |
     1 FW (AD)          328 FW (AD)             |
    ___|_____        |                    |
   |       |       |     71 FIS              27 FIS
 DC Ops  DC Mat  1 CSG
   |       |    ___|___
 94 FIS  1 CMS |       |
             1 CES   1 APS
              |       |
             1 SS    1 TS
              |       |
            WAFS   HQ & HQ
                   Sq Sect
```

Appendix III-13

Organization
1 October 1970

On 1 October 1970 Headquarters, Tactical Air Command activated the 1st Tactical Fighter Wing at MacDill AFB, Florida. The wing absorbed the five flying squadrons previously assigned the 15th Tactical Fighter Wing at MacDill at this time. This organization, governed by TACR 23-67, placed the maintenance, supply, and flying squadrons directly under the wing commander. The operations and materiel directorates essentially supervised staff offices, not support units.

Abbreviations

AF	Air Force
AD	Air Division
CCTS	Combat Crew Training Squadron
CES	Civil Engineering Squadron
CSG	Combat Support Group
Dir	Directorate
FMS	Field Maintenance Squadron
Hosp	Hospital
HQ Sq Sect	Headquarters Squadron Section
Mat	Materiel
Ops	Operations
Rgnl	Regional
SPS	Security Police Squadron
SVS	Services Squadron
SS	Supply Squadron
TAC	Tactical Air Command
Tac	Tactical
TFS	Tactical Fighter Squadron
TFW	Tactical Fighter Wing
TRS	Transportation Squadron
TTS	Tactical Training Squadron

Appendix III-13

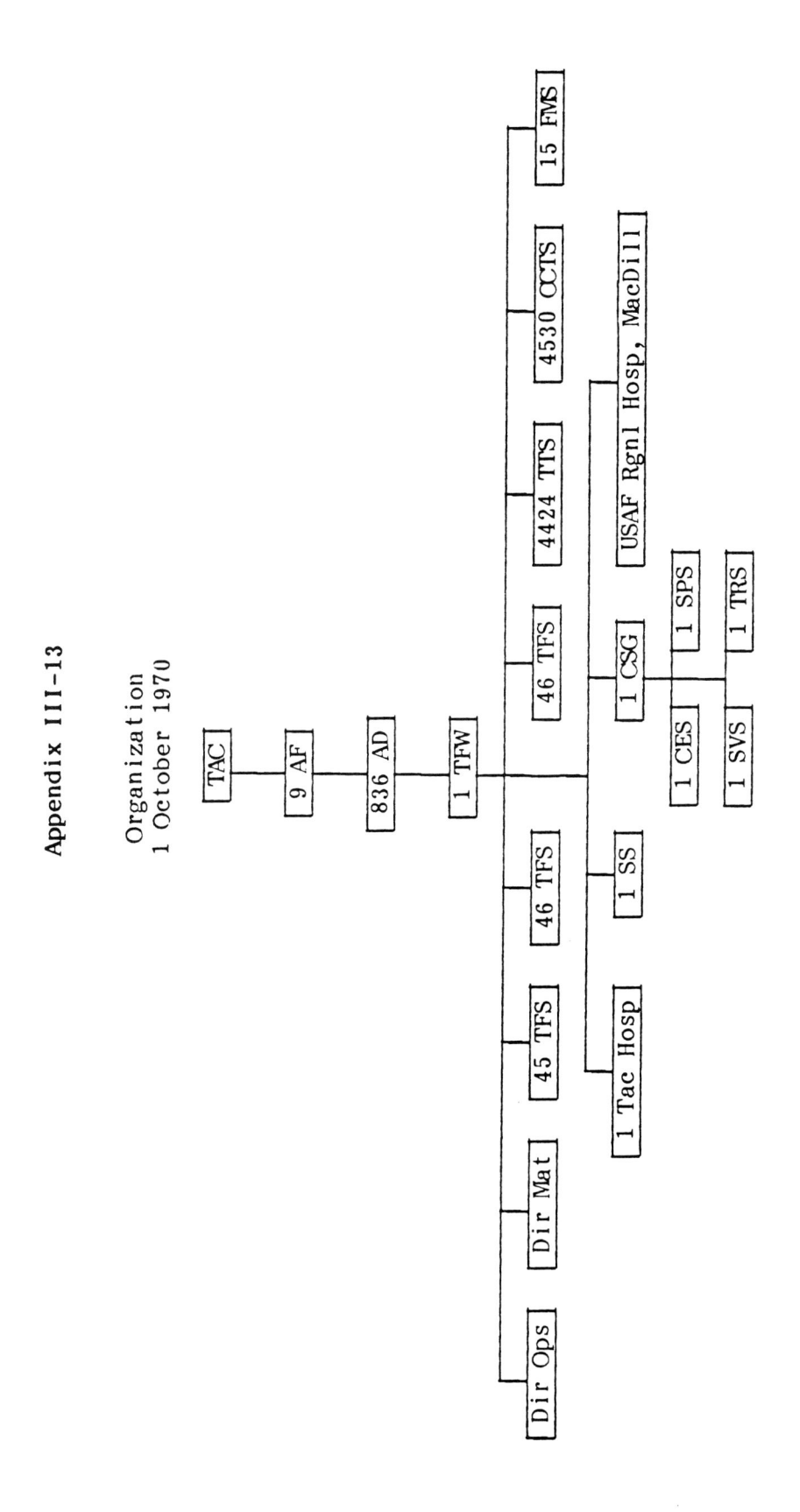

Organization
1 October 1970

```
TAC
 │
9 AF
 │
836 AD
 │
1 TFW
 ├── Dir Ops
 ├── Dir Mat
 ├── 45 TFS
 ├── 46 TFS
 ├── 46 TFS
 ├── 4424 TTS
 ├── 4530 CCTS
 ├── 15 FMS
 ├── 1 Tac Hosp
 ├── 1 SS
 └── 1 CSG
      ├── 1 CES
      ├── 1 SVS
      ├── 1 SPS
      ├── 1 TRS
      └── USAF Rgnl Hosp, MacDill
```

Appendix III-14

Organization
1 July 1971

On 1 July 1971, TAC assigned the 27th, 71st, and 94th tactical fighter squadrons to the 1st Tactical Fighter Wing. Except for the redesignation of the three fighter squadrons, the wing's basic organization remained essentially unchanged. The wing was, however, relieved from its assignment to the 836th Air Division and assigned to Ninth Air Force on the inactivation of the division on 1 July 1971.

Abbreviations

AF	Air Force
AD	Air Division
CCTS	Combat Crew Training Squadron
CES	Civil Engineering Squadron
CSG	Combat Support Group
Dir	Directorate
FMS	Field Maintenance Squadron
Hosp	Hospital
HQ Sq Sect	Headquarters Squadron Section
Mat	Materiel
Ops	Operations
Rgnl	Regional
SPS	Security Police Squadron
SVS	Services Squadron
SS	Supply Squadron
TAC	Tactical Air Command
Tac	Tactical
TFS	Tactical Fighter Squadron
TFW	Tactical Fighter Wing
TRS	Transportation Squadron
TTS	Tactical Training Squadron

Appendix III-14

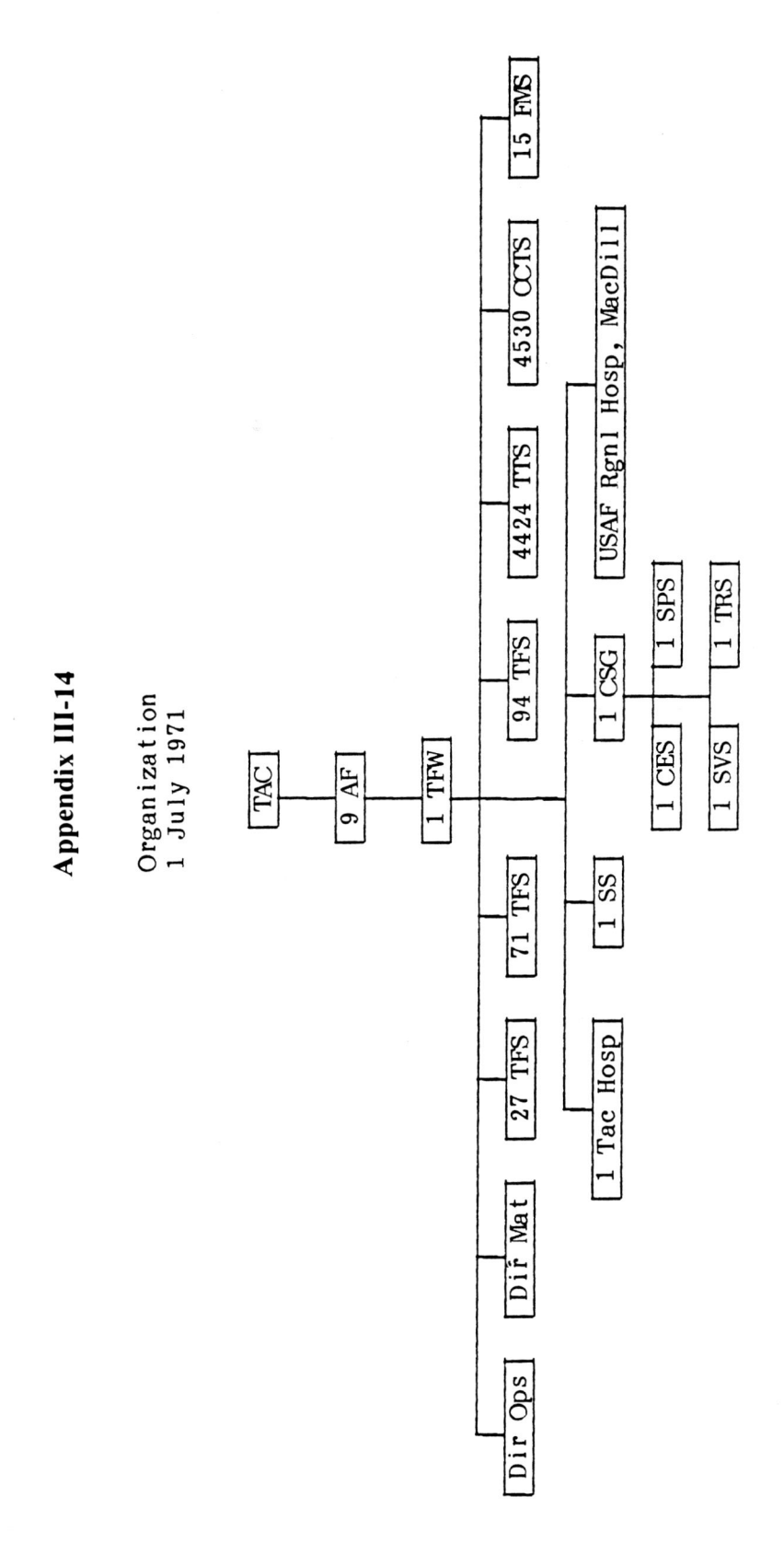

Organization
1 July 1971

```
                                    TAC
                                     |
                                    9 AF
                                     |
                                   1 TFW
    ┌──────────┬──────────┬─────────┼─────────┬──────────┬──────────┬──────────┐
  Dir Ops   Dir Mat    27 TFS    71 TFS    94 TFS    4424 TTS   4530 CCTS   15 FMS
                                             |
                                           1 CSG
                                             |
              ┌──────────┬──────────┬────────┼────────┬──────────┬──────────┐
          1 Tac Hosp   1 SS      1 CES    1 SVS    1 SPS      1 TRS    USAF Rgnl Hosp, MacDill
```

Appendix III-15

Organization
19 April 1976

TAC moved the 1st Tactical Fighter Wing to Langley AFB, Virginia, on 30 June 1975. By 19 April 1976, with the assignment of the 6th Airborne Command and Control Squadron, the operational side of the wing had assumed the form it would carry into the 1980's. The 1st Combat Support Group and its squadrons were, however, not part of the wing at this time. The 4500th Air Base Wing served as host unit at Langley and provided the services for which the 1st CSG would otherwise have been responsible. The creation of the tri-deputy system in 1975 put the flying and support squadrons under deputy commanders; they no longer reported directly to the wing commander.

Abbreviations

ACCS	Airborne Command and Control Squadron
AF	Air Force
AMS	Avionics Maintenance Squadron
DCO	Deputy Commander for Operations
DCM	Deputy Commander for Maintenance
DCR	Deputy Commander for Resources
FMS	Field Maintenance Squadron
MMS	Munitions Maintenance Squadron
OMS	Organizational Maintenance Squadron
TAC	Tactical Air Command
TFS	Tactical Fighter Squadron
TFW	Tactical Fighter Wing

Appendix III-15

Organization
19 April 1976

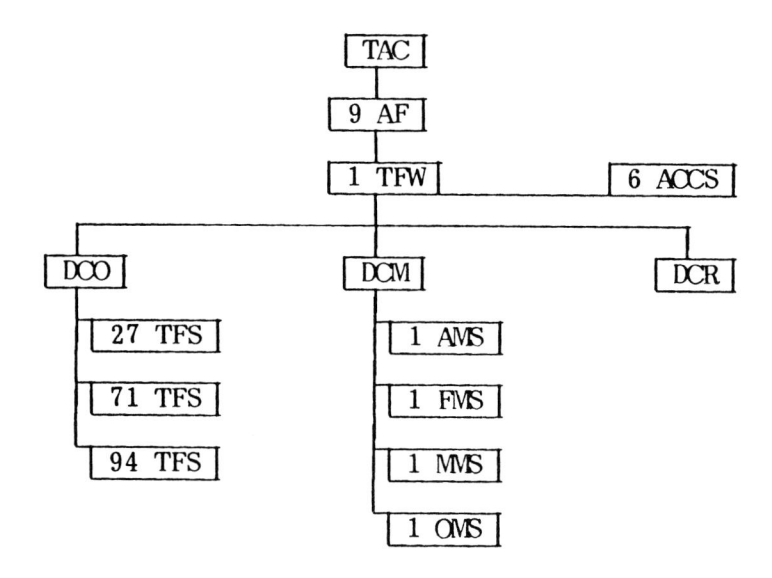

```
                    ┌─────┐
                    │ TAC │
                    └──┬──┘
                    ┌──┴──┐
                    │ 9 AF│
                    └──┬──┘
                    ┌──┴──┐           ┌────────┐
                    │1 TFW├───────────┤ 6 ACCS │
                    └──┬──┘           └────────┘
         ┌────────────┼────────────┐
      ┌──┴──┐      ┌──┴──┐      ┌──┴──┐
      │ DCO │      │ DCM │      │ DCR │
      └──┬──┘      └──┬──┘      └─────┘
    ┌────┴───┐    ┌───┴────┐
    │ 27 TFS │    │ 1 AMS  │
    └────────┘    └────────┘
    ┌────────┐    ┌────────┐
    │ 71 TFS │    │ 1 FMS  │
    └────────┘    └────────┘
    ┌────────┐    ┌────────┐
    │ 94 TFS │    │ 1 MMS  │
    └────────┘    └────────┘
                  ┌────────┐
                  │ 1 OMS  │
                  └────────┘
```

Appendix III-16

Organization
15 June 1977

With the activation of the 1st Combat Support Group on 15 April 1977 and the reorganization of the maintenance complex two months later, the 1st Tactical Fighter Wing assumed all the major elements of its contemporary organization.

Abbreviations

ACCS	Airborne Command and Control Squadron
AF	Air Force
AGS	Aircraft Generation Squadron
CES	Civil Engineering Squadron
CRS	Component Repair Squadron
CSG	Combat Support Group
DCM	Deputy Commander for Maintenance
DCO	Deputy Commander for Operations
DCR	Deputy Commander for Resource Management
EMS	Equipment Maintenance Squadron
SPS	Security Police Squadron
SUP	Supply Squadron
SVS	Services Squadron
TAC	Tactical Air Command
TFS	Tactical Fighter Squadron
TFW	Tactical Fighter Wing

Appendix III-16

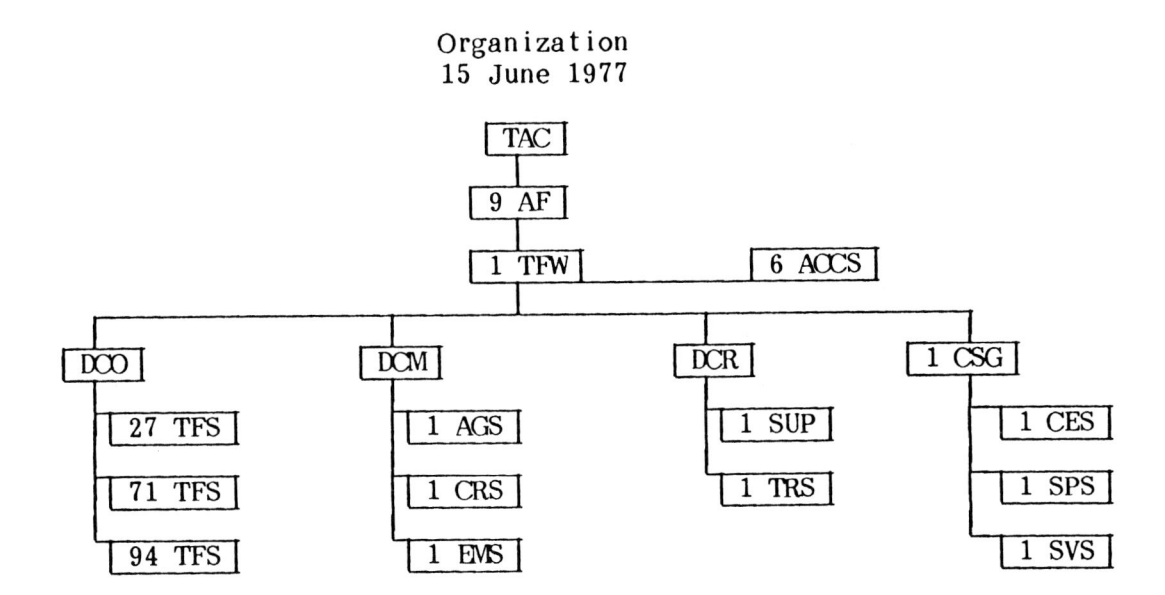

Organization
15 June 1977

```
                    TAC
                     |
                    9 AF
                     |
         ┌──────── 1 TFW ──── 6 ACCS
         |
   ┌─────┼─────┬─────────┬─────────┐
  DCO   DCM   DCR      1 CSG
   |     |     |         |
 27 TFS 1 AGS 1 SUP    1 CES
 71 TFS 1 CRS 1 TRS    1 SPS
 94 TFS 1 EMS          1 SVS
```

Appendix III-17

Organization
5 May 1983

This chart outlines the complete organization of the 1st Tactical Fighter Wing on its 65th anniversary. It includes the major staff offices in addition to the operational and support squadrons.

Abbreviations

AC	Comptroller	EMS	Equipment Maintenance Squadron
ACCS	Airborne Command & Control Sq	HC	Chaplain
AGS	Aircraft Generation Squadron	HO	History Office
CCQ	Headquarters Squadron Section	JA	Judge Advocate
CES	Civil Engineering Squadron	LGC	Contracting
CRS	Component Repair Squadron	LGX	Resource Planning
CSG	Combat Support Group	MAM	Maintenance Control
DA	Administration	MAQ	Quality Assurance
DCM	Dep Commander for Maintenance	MAS	Maintenance Management
DCO	Dep Commander for Operations	MAT	Maintenance Training
DCR	Dep Cmdr for Resource Mgmt	PA	Public Affairs
DOA	Operations Administration	SE	Safety
DOC	Command Post	SG	Surgeon
DOF	Helicopter Operations	SL	Social Actions
DOI	Intelligence Division	SPS	Security Police Squadron
DOT	Operations Training	SS	Morale, Welfare, and Recreation
DOV	Standardization & Evaluation	SUP	Supply Squadron
DOW	Weapons and Tactics	SVS	Services Squadron
DOX	Operations Plans	TFS	Tactical Fighter Squadron
DP	Personnel	TFW	Tactical Fighter Wing
DW	Disaster Preparedness	TRS	Transportation Squadron

Appendix III-17

Organization
5 May 1983

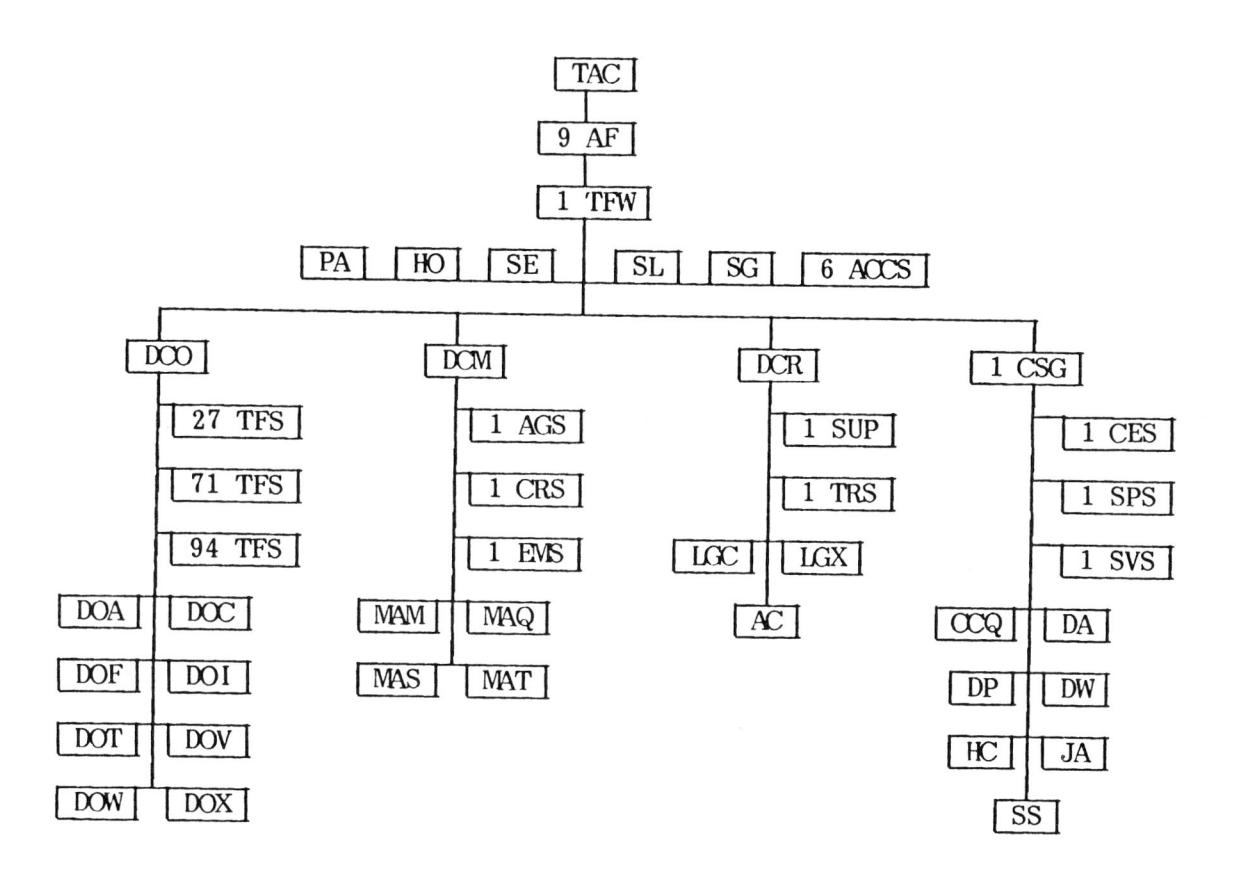

```
                            ┌─────┐
                            │ TAC │
                            └──┬──┘
                            ┌──┴──┐
                            │ 9 AF│
                            └──┬──┘
                            ┌──┴──┐
                            │1 TFW│
                            └──┬──┘
   ┌──────┬──────┬───────┬───┼────┬──────┐
 ┌─┴┐  ┌──┴┐  ┌──┴┐   ┌──┴┐ ┌┴─┐ ┌┴──────┐
 │PA│  │HO │  │SE │   │SL │ │SG│ │6 ACCS │
 └──┘  └───┘  └───┘   └───┘ └──┘ └───────┘
       ┌──────────┬──────────┬──────────┐
    ┌──┴┐      ┌──┴┐      ┌──┴┐      ┌──┴──┐
    │DCO│      │DCM│      │DCR│      │1 CSG│
    └─┬─┘      └─┬─┘      └─┬─┘      └──┬──┘
  ┌───┴──┐   ┌───┴──┐   ┌───┴──┐    ┌───┴──┐
  │27 TFS│   │1 AGS │   │1 SUP │    │1 CES │
  └──────┘   └──────┘   └──────┘    └──────┘
  ┌──────┐   ┌──────┐   ┌──────┐    ┌──────┐
  │71 TFS│   │1 CRS │   │1 TRS │    │1 SPS │
  └──────┘   └──────┘   └──────┘    └──────┘
  ┌──────┐   ┌──────┐   ┌───┐┌───┐  ┌──────┐
  │94 TFS│   │1 EMS │   │LGC││LGX│  │1 SVS │
  └──────┘   └──────┘   └───┘└───┘  └──────┘
 ┌───┐┌───┐ ┌───┐┌───┐    ┌──┐      ┌───┐┌──┐
 │DOA││DOC│ │MAM││MAQ│    │AC│      │CCQ││DA│
 └───┘└───┘ └───┘└───┘    └──┘      └───┘└──┘
 ┌───┐┌───┐ ┌───┐┌───┐              ┌───┐┌──┐
 │DOF││DOI│ │MAS││MAT│              │DP ││DW│
 └───┘└───┘ └───┘└───┘              └───┘└──┘
 ┌───┐┌───┐                         ┌───┐┌──┐
 │DOT││DOV│                         │HC ││JA│
 └───┘└───┘                         └───┘└──┘
 ┌───┐┌───┐                           ┌──┐
 │DOW││DOX│                           │SS│
 └───┘└───┘                           └──┘
```

Appendix IV

Appendix IV

Group/Wing Commanders
1918 - 1983

Group Commanders
1918 - 1955

Maj Bert M. Atkinson, 5 May 1918
Maj Harold E. Hartney, 21 Aug 1918
LtCol Davenport Johnson, Aug 1919
Capt Arthur R. Brooks
Maj Carl Spaatz, Nov 1921
Maj Thomas G. Lanphier
Maj Ralph Royce, 1928
LtCol Charles H. Danforth, 1930
Maj George H. Brett
LtCol Frank M. Andrews, Jul 1933
LtCol Ralph Royce, 1934
Maj Edwin J. House, 30 Apr 1937
Col Henry B. Clagett, 1938
Col Lawrence P. Hickey, 1939
LtCol Robert S. Israel, Jul 1941
Maj John O. Zahn, 1 May 1942
Col John N. Stone, 9 Jul 1942
Col Ralph S. Garman, 7 Dec 1942
Maj Joseph H. Preddie, 8 Sep 1943
Col Robert B. Richard, 19 Sep 1943
Col Arthur C. Agan, Jr., 15 Nov 1944
Col Milton H. Ashkins, 31 Mar 1945
LtCol Charles W. Thaxton, 11 Apr 1945
Col Milton H. Ashkins, 28 Apr 1945
Col Bruce K. Holloway, 3 Jul 1946
Col Gilbert L. Meyers, 20 Aug 1946
Col Frank S. Perego, Jan 1948
LtCol Jack T. Bradley, Jul 1950
Col Dolf E. Muehleisen, Jun 1951
Col Walker M. Mahurin, 1951
Capt Robert B. Bell, Jan 1952
Col Norman S. Orwat, 1955

Wing Commanders
1947-1983

Col Carl J. Crane, 15 Aug 1947
Col Elvin F. Maughn, 19 Jan 1948
Col Clifford H. Rees, 17 May 1948
Col Joseph H. Davidson, 13 Jan 1949
Col George McCoy, Jr., 14 Jun 1949
Col William M. Lee, 19 Aug 1949
Col Wiley D. Ganey, 4 Jan 1950
Col George McCoy, Jr., 17 Feb 1950
Brig Gen Donald R. Hutchinson, 17 Oct 1950
Col Dolf E. Muehleisen, Dec 1950
Col Robert F. Worley, Jun 1951
Col Glenn E. Duncan, 18 Oct 1956
Col Charles D. Sonkalb, Aug 1959
Col George J. LeBreche, Dec 1960
Col Ralph G. Taylor, Jr., 15 Jun 1962
Col Wallace B. Frank, 11 Sep 1963
Col Converse B. Kelly, 16 Sep 1963
Col Kenneth E. Rosebush, Aug 1966
Col Tarras T. Popovich, 29 Apr 1968
Col Morris B. Pitts, Oct 1969
Col Mervin M. Taylor, Jan 1970
Col Travis R. McNeill, 1 Oct 1970
Col Robert F. Titus, 1 Mar 1971
Col Howard D. Leaf, 6 May 1971
Col Walter D. Duren, Jr., 1 Nov 71
Col Sydney L. Davis, 18 Apr 1972
Col Gerald J. Carey, Jr., 25 Jun 1973
Col Ernest A. Bedke, Jun 1975
LtCol George H. Miller, 1 Jul 1975
Brig Gen Larry D. Welch, 1 Aug 1975
Col John T. Chain, 1 Aug 1977
Col Neil L. Eddins, 27 Mar 78
Col Donald L. Miller, 15 May 1979
Brig Gen William T. Tolbert, 11 Aug 1980
Col Eugene H. Fischer, 29 Jan 1982
Col Henry Viccellio, Jr., 6 Apr 1983

CHAPTER ONE

[1] James S. Alford, "The History of the 1st Pursuit Group" (Ms, 2 vols, 1st Tactical Fighter Wing History Office), Volume I, The 1st Pursuit Group in World War I (1959), p 4 (hereafter cited as Alford, History, I); "1st Pursuit Group Diary, 1918-1937" (Ms, 2 vols, 1st Tactical Fighter Wing History Office), Volume I, 1918, p 1 (hereafter cited as Diary, I); James J. Hudson, Hostile Skies: A Combat History of the American Air Service in World War I (Syracuse, NY: Syracuse University Press, 1968), pp 53, 63-64 (hereafter cited as Hudson, Hostile Skies).

[2] Alford, History, I, pp 4-5.

[3] Ibid.

[4] Mauer Mauer, ed., The U.S. Air Service in World War I, 4 vols (Washington: Office of Air Force History, 1978-1979), Volume I, "Tactical History of the Air Service," p 283 (hereafter cited as USAS in WWI); Alford, History, I, pp 6-8.

[5] Diary, I, pp 25-28.

[6] Alford, History, I, p 8; Diary, I, pp 36, 38.

[7] Hudson, Hostile Skies, pp 64-65; Diary, I, p 38.

[8] Diary, I, p 38; Edward V. Rickenbacker, Rickenbacker, An Autobiography (Englewood Cliffs, NJ: Prentice-Hall, Inc, 1967), pp 97-100 (hereafter cited as Rickenbacker, Autobiography); Edward V. Rickenbacker, Fighting the Flying Circus (Garden City, NY: Doubleday & Co., Inc., 1965), pp 3-8 (hereafter cited as Rickenbacker, Flying Circus).

[9] Diary, I, p 39; Alford, History, I, pp 9-10.

[10] Diary, I, pp 39-40.

[11] Rickenbacker, Flying Circus, p 16; Alford, History, I, p 13; Diary, I, pp 40-41.

[12] Diary, I, pp 42-44; Alford, History, I, p 13; USAS WWI, I, p 283; Hudson, Hostile Skies, p 66.

[13] Alford, History, I, p 15; Diary, I, p 44.

[14] USAS WWI, I, p 283.

[15] Ibid.

[16] Rickenbacker, Flying Circus, p 15.

[17] Alford, History, I, p 16.

[18] USAS WWI, I, pp 283-284.

[19] Diary, I, p 46; Alford, History, I, pp 16-17; Rickenbacker, Autobiography, p 102; Rickenbacker, Flying Circus, pp 16-22; USAS WWI, I, pp 31, 284; Hudson, Hostile Skies, pp 1-2.

[20] Rickenbacker, Flying Circus, pp 22-28; Alford, History, I, p 18; Diary, I, p 49.

[21] Diary, I, pp 24-42; Alford, History, I, pp 41-42; Harold E. Hartney, Up and At 'Em (New York: Arno Press, 1980; reprint of 1940 Stackpile edition), pp 103, 106-107 (hereafter cited as Hartney, At 'Em).

[22] Diary, I, pp. 28-48.

[23] Alford, History, I, p 28; Diary, I, p 51; USAS WWI, I, p 285.

[24] Alford, History, I, p 28; Diary, I, p 51.

[25] Alford, History, I, pp 20-26, 34-35; Diary, I, pp 56-60.

[26] Diary, I, pp 60-61. The letter is undated.

[27] Alford, History, I, p 33.

[28] Diary, I, pp 65-66; Alford, History, I, pp 40, 47-48; USAS WWI, I, p 285; Rickenbacker, Flying Circus, pp 97-99; Hudson, Hostile Skies, pp 76-77.

[29] Diary, I, pp 74-76.

[30] Hartney, At 'Em, p 243.

[31] USAS WWI, I, p 291.

[32] Ibid.

[33] Ibid.; Hudson, Hostile Skies, p 92.

[34] Hudson, Hostile Skies, p 92; Alford, History, I, p 58.

[35] Hudson, Hostile Skies, p 92.

[36] USAS WWI, I, p 292.

[37] Alford, History, I, p 60.

[38] USAS WWI, I, p 292.

Notes, pages 9-12

[39] Ibid., p 293.

[40] Hudson, Hostile Skies, pp 95-97.

[41] Hartney, At 'Em, pp 159, 196, 198.

[42] Ibid., p 196; USAS WWI, I, p 295.

[43] Hudson, Hostile Skies, pp 101-102, 110-111, 113-114; Hartney, At 'Em, p 243.

[44] USAS WWI, I, p 299.

[45] Ibid.

[46] Diary, I, p 98; Hartney, At 'Em, pp 200-202; Hudson, Hostile Skies, p 122.

[47] USAS WWI, I, p 305; Alford, History, I, p 102; Hudson, Hostile Skies, p 140.

[48] USAS WWI, I, pp 307-309; III, p 138-139.

[49] Diary, I, p 111.

[50] Ibid., p 115; Rickenbacker, Autobiography, p 125; Rickenbacker, Flying Circus, p 205.

[51] Hudson, Hostile Skies, pp 260-261.

[52] Rickenbacker, Flying Circus, p 205.

[53] Ibid., pp 205-206.

[54] Ibid.

[55] Ibid., p 206.

[56] Hartney, At 'Em, p 243.

[57] Ibid., p 203.

[58] Ibid., p 243.

[59] USAS WWI, I, p 319.

[60] Hudson, Hostile Skies, p 260.

[61] USAS WWI, I, p 319.

[62] Diary, I, p 86.

[63] Hartney, At 'Em, pp 250-288.

[64] Ibid.; War Department General Order 59, 1919.

[65] Diary, I, p 28; Hartney, At 'Em, p 233; Hudson, Hostile Skies, pp 283-286.

[66] Alford, History, I, p 183; Diary, I, p 151; Hudson, Hostile Skies, p 294.

[67] Hudson, Hostile Skies, pp 307-311; Hartney, At 'Em, p 243. For many years, Rickenbacker, Luke, and Lufbery were listed as America's top-scoring aces in World War I. In recent years, greater credit has gone to Americans who served with the British and French throughout the war. The list of "Leading American Aces of World War I" that appeared in the May 1986 issue of Air Force magazine relegates Luke and Lufbery to eighth and ninth place, respectively:

Rickenbacker, Capt Edward V. (AEF)	26 Kills
Lambert, Capt William C. (Royal Flying Corps - RFC)	22 "
Gillette, Capt Frederick W. (RFC)	20 "
Malone, Capt John J. (Royal Navy)	20 "
Wilkinson, Maj Alan M. (RFC)	19 "
Hale, Capt Frank L. (RFC)	18 "
Iaccaci, Capt Paul T. (RFC)	18 "
Luke, 2Lt Frank, Jr. (AEF)	18 "
Lufbery, Maj Raoul G. (AEF)	17 "

[68] Diary, I, pp 152-160; 1st Pursuit Group Diary, Volume II, 1919-1937, pp 185-193 (hereafter cited as Diary, II).

CHAPTER TWO

[1] "1st Pursuit Group Diary, 1917-1937," (Ms, 2 vols, 1st Tactical Fighter Wing History Office), Volume II, 1919-1937, pp 185-195 (hereafter cited as Diary, II); Mauer Mauer, ed., Air Force Combat Units of World War II (Maxwell AFB, AL: USAF Historical Division, Air University, 1960), pp 21-24; Charles A. Ravenstein, Organization of the Air Force (Maxwell AFB, AL: Research Division, Albert F. Simpson Historical Research Center, 1982), pp 6-8. For lineage purposes, the group organized at Selfridge was not related to the World War I group. The connection between the two groups was not made until 1924, when the World War I headquarters was reconstituted and consolidated with the 1919 Selfridge group. This action, authorized by War Department Circular No. 25, 8 April 1924, enabled the group to trace its lineage back to World War I. For more on the lineage process, see Mauer, AF Combat Units, World War II, pp 1-5, 475-477; Charles A. Ravenstein, Lineage and Honors Histories: Their Parts, and Problems in Preparing (Maxwell AFB, AL: AFSHRC, Air University, 1975).

[2] Diary, II, p 205.

[3] Robert Frank Futrell, Ideas, Concepts, Doctrine: A History of Basic Thinking in the United States Air Force, 1907-1964 (Maxwell AFB, AL: Air University, 1971), pp 15-17.

[4] Course of Study, 1st Pursuit Group Advanced Course of Training, Operations Order 93, 15 April 1921, GP-1-SU-OP(FTR) in USAF Collection, USAF Historical Research Center (USAFHRC).

[5] Ibid.

[6] Diary, II, pp 208-209.

[7] "Selfridge Air National Guard Base, An Unofficial History," Ms, nd.

[8] James S. Alford, "The History of the 1st Pursuit Group," (Ms, 2 vols, 1959, 1961), Vol II, 1919-1960, pp 8-9 (hereafter cited as Alford, History, II); Souvenir Program, Mitchell Trophy Air Races, 17 October 1936, Selfridge Field, Michigan.

[9] These periodic inspections are at least mentioned, and often described in some detail, in the Diary, II, passim.

[10] Diary, II, p 217; Alford, History, II, p 13; Short History, Coat of Arms, 1st Fighter Group, in USAF Collection, USAFSHRC.

[11] Diary, II, p 217.

[12] Diary, II, pp 218, 221-223.

[13] The Oscoda camp is first mentioned in Diary, II, p 217. The date of first use is not recorded.

[14] Diary, II, pp 225-233. The dawn-to-dusk flight is discussed on pp 226-227.

[15] Program, Air Service Demonstration, Langley Field, Virginia, for Congressional Select Committee, 6 March 1925, 248.2126 in USAF Collection, USAFSHRC.

[16] Diary, II, pp 227, 229-230.

[17] Ibid., pp 230-233.

[18] Ibid., pp 234-236; Report, Brig Gen J. E. Fechet, Assistant Chief of Staff, Air Service, to AGO, 17 May 1926; subj: Maneuvers of the Army Air Service, 1926, 248.2122 in USAF Collection, USAFHRC.

[19] Fechet Report, 17 May 26, pp 2-9.

[20] Diary, II, pp 236-244.

[21] "Report of Winter Maneuvers - 1st Pursuit Group, A.C., January 24, 1927 to January 30, 1927," p 1, GP-1-SU-OP(FTR) in USAF Collection, USAFHRC.

[22] "Report of Winter Maneuvers, 1927," pp 2-4.

[23] Ibid., pp 4-5.

[24] Ibid., pp 5-6.

[25] Ibid., p 6.

[26] Ibid.

[27] Ibid., pp 6-7.

[28] Ibid., pp 8-12.

[29] Diary, II, pp 245-246.

[30] Ibid., pp 247-249.

[31] Ibid., p 250.

[32] Remarks by Brig Gen James E. Fechet, Critique of 1927 Maneuvers, 20 May 1927, p 7; also see Hq VIII Corps Area, Maneuver Memorandums Nos 1 and 7, 18 April and 14 May 1927, and Report of Brig Gen LeRoy Elting, 19 May 1927, in Critique of 1927 Maneuvers, 20 May 1927, p 5, all in Air Corps Maneuvers, 1926-1943, 248.2122 in USAF Collection, USAFHRC.

[33] Diary, II, p 250.

Notes, pages 25-29

34 Ibid., pp 252-253.

35 Mauer, Combat Squadrons, WWII, p 317; Alford, History, II, p 17.

36 Operations Orders 1 and 3, 1 and 2 May 1928, Air Corps Demonstration Group, Langley Field, in Army Air Corps Maneuvers, 248.2122 in USAF Collection, USAFHRC; Diary, II, pp 261-164.

37 Diary, II, pp 262-264.

38 Ibid., pp 264-269.

39 Critique delivered by Maj W. H. Frank at Wright Field, OH, 26 May 1929, in Army Air Corps Maneuvers, 1926-1943, 248.2122, in USAF Collection, USAFHRC.

40 Ibid.

41 Diary, II, pp 272-286.

42 For information on the types of aircraft that the group used, see Ken C. Rust, "Aces and Hawks: History of the 1st Fighter Wing," Part I, 1918-1939, Airpower Historian, Vol IX, No 4, October 1962, p 222. For technical information, see Lloyd S. Jones, U.S. Fighters (Fallbrook, CA: Aero Publishers, Inc., 1975), pp 11-13.

43 Diary, II, p 288; Artic Patrol Flight of the 1st Pursuit Group, US Army Air Corps, Official Log, 8-29 January 1930, in The Service News, Vol 7, No 4, 15 Feb 30, pp 6-17, GP-1-SU-NE(FTR) in USAF Collection, USAFHRC (hereafter cited as APF Log). The quotes are from APF Log, p 6.

44 APF Log, p 7.

45 Ibid., pp 7-10.

46 Ibid., pp 11-12.

47 Ibid., pp 13-16.

48 Diary, II, pp 300-304.

49 Ibid., pp 305-307.

50 Ibid., pp 316, 347; Mauer, Combat Squadrons, pp 171-172.

51 Diary, II, p 320.

52 Ibid., p 325.

[53] Ibid., pp 326-328.

[54] Ibid., pp 334-335; 362-388.

[55] Ibid., p 347.

[56] Normal training activities are listed in detail in Diary, II, passim.

[57] Jones, US Fighters, pp 26-31, 42-45.

[58] Ibid., pp 50-51.

[59] Diary, II, pp 355-357.

[60] Ibid., pp 357-358.

[61] Ibid., pp 358-361.

[62] Ibid., pp 363-364.

[63] Ibid., p 370.

[64] Ibid., p 371.

[65] Ibid., pp 373-377.

[66] Ibid., pp 373, 375.

[67] Ibid., pp 380-388; Jones, US Fighters, pp 68-70.

[68] Diary, II, p 384.

[69] Ibid., pp 384-385.

[70] Ibid., pp 390-391.

[71] Ravenstein, Organization of the Air Force, p 7.

[72] Diary, II, pp 395-397.

[73] Ibid., pp 401-402.

[74] Ibid., pp 412-422.

[75] Ibid., p 423.

[76] Much of this information was compiled from Alford, History, I & II, and the Diary, I &

II. Most of the references take the form of almost off-handed comments about support functions. These activities are covered in more detail from the World War II period onward.

[77] Diary, II, p 427; Program, Mitchell Trophy Air Races, 17 October 1936, in 1st Tactical Fighter Wing History Office files.

[78] Diary, II, p 431.

[79] Ibid.

[80] Jones, US Fighters, pp 82-87.

[81] Ibid., p 82.

[82] Diary, II, pp 434-436.

[83] Ibid., pp 436-443.

[84] 1st Tactical Fighter Wing History Office files contain an article by Dana Bell entitled "Purple and Orange," which describes these schemes. There is no identification of the source of this article, although it may have come from an International Plastic Modelers Society publication.

[85] Mauer, Combat Squadrons, pp 94-96.

[86] Hist, 71st Fighter Squadron, 1 Jan 41-30 Apr 43, SQ-FI71-HI in USAF Collection, USAFHRC; Mauer, Combat Squadrons, pp 261-262. For information on the 1941 maneuvers, see Christopher R. Gabel, "The 1941 GHQ Maneuvers," Ph.D. dissertation, The Ohio State University, 1981.

[87] Jones, US Fighters, p 91.

[88] Ibid., pp 68-709 for the P-26; 91-94 for the P-38.

[89] Alford, History, II, p 34.

CHAPTER THREE

[1] James S. Alford, "The History of the 1st Pursuit Group", (Ms, 2 vols, 1959, 1961), Volume II, The 1st Fighter Group in World War II, p 35 (hereafter cited as Alford, History, II), War Diary, 1st Fighter Group, 7 Dec 41-15 Jan 44, GP-1-SU-RE-D(FTR) in USAF Collection, USAFHRC, pp 1-2 (hereafter cited as War Diary); Kit C. Carter and Robert Mueller, comps., The Army Air Forces in World War II - Combat Chronology, 1941 - 1945 (Maxwell AFB, AL: AFSHRC and HQ USAF Office of Air Force History, 1973), p 2 (hereafter cited as Combat Chronology).

[2] Ltr, 1Lt Frederick C. Crambo, Cmdr, 71st Pursuit, to Major Robert S. Israel, Jr., Cmdr, 1st Pursuit Group, 20 Dec 41, in Short History of 1st Fighter Group Coat of Arms and Flags, GP-1-HI(FTR) in USAF Collection, USAFHRC.

[3] War Diary, pp 4-5; Alford, History, II, pp 38-39.

[4] Edward V. Rickenbacker, Rickenbacker: An Autobiography (Englewood Cliffs, NJ: Prentice-Hall, Inc., 1967), pp 272-273.

[5] Ibid., p 277.

[6] Ibid., pp 276-277.

[7] Ibid., p 274.

[8] Ibid.

[9] Ibid.

[10] Wesley F. Craven and James L. Cate, The Army Air Forces in World War II, Vol I, Plans and Early Operations, January 1939 to August 1942 (Chicago, IL: The University of Chicago Press, 1948), pp 564-566, 574-576, 652-653.

[11] Ltr, Maj Gen D. D. Eisenhower, Asst Chief of Staff, to various, OPD 370.5, 23 April 1942, and Movement Orders, Air Echelon, 1st Pursuit Group (Fighter), AGO 370.5 MC-E-M, 14 May 1942, in Bolero Plans (Books I & II), 168.603.110(S), in USAF Collection, USAFHRC; Alford, History, II, pp 38-39; War Diary, pp 7-8.

[12] Alford, History, II, pp 40-41; War Diary, p 9.

[13] Bolero Ferry Plan, 168.7032-78 in USAF Collection, USAFHRC.

[14] Ibid.

[15] Combat Chronology, p 19; Alford, History, II, p 42.

[16] Alford, History, II, p 42.

[17] Air Route Manual, United States to Great Britain, 29 July 1942, Inclosure 1 to Annex 2, Bolero Training Directive, 1 August 1942, pp 59-61, in Bolero Training Directives, 244.213, in USAF Collection, USAFHRC.

[18] Ibid., pp 63-71. The quote is from p 68.

[19] Alford, History, II, p 44.

[20] Alford, History, II, pp 47-51; Combat Chronology, p 29, Bolero Aircraft Status Reports in Bolero Files, 520.2131, in USAF Collection, USAFHRC.

[21] Combat Chronology, pp 32-33; Alford, History, II, pp 48-49; AFSHRC, USAF Credits for the Destruction of Enemy Aircraft, World War II, USAF Historical Study No 85 (Maxwell AFB, AL: AFSHRC, 1978), p 539 (hereafter cited as Combat Kills, WWII).

[22] Alford, History, II, p 51; War Diary, p 10.

[23] Alford, History, II, p 53.

[24] Ibid., p 52.

[25] Ibid., pp 53-54; Diary, 71st Fighter Squadron, 1 January 1941-30 April 1943, SQ-FI-71-HI in USAF Collection, USAFHRC (hereafter cited as 71st Diary).

[26] War Diary (no pagination after about p 10).

[27] Alford, History, II, p 57.

[28] War Diary; Alford, History, II, pp 58, 62; 71st Diary, entry for 27 Nov 42.

[29] 71st Diary, entry for 27 Nov 42.

[30] Alford, History, II, pp 61-63; the quote is from p 63.

[31] Ibid., pp 66-69; War Diary, entry for 7 Dec 42; 71st Diary, entries for 4 Dec 42, 25 Dec 42. The quote is from the 25 Dec entry.

[32] Alford, History, II, pp 72-77.

[33] Ibid., p 72.

[34] Ibid., p 73.

[35] Ibid., pp 72-74.

[36] War Diary, entry for 1 January 1943.

[37] Alford, History, II, p 129.

[38] Ibid.

[39] Ibid., p 76; War Diary, entry for 7 Jan 43.

[40] War Diary, entries for 10 and 15 Jan 43. The quote is from the 15 Jan entry.

[41] Alford, History, II, pp 79-87; War Diary, entry for 10 Feb 43.

[42] Alford, History, II, p 88; War Diary, entry for 10 Apr 43; 71st Diary, entry for 10 Apr 43.

[43] Alford, History, II, p 89.

[44] 71st Diary, entry for 1 Aug 43.

[45] Ibid., entry for 24 Aug 43.

[46] War Department General Order 66, 1944.

[47] Ibid.

[48] Alford, History, II, pp 119-122.

[49] 71st Diary, entry for 25 Aug 43.

[50] War Department General Order 66, 1944.

[51] War Department General Order 44, 1946; 71st Diary, entry for 30 August 1943; War Diary, entry for 30 August 43; Alford, History, II, pp 131-136. This DUC was actually the group's third; the second was awarded in 1944 for action on 18 May 1944. See below.

[52] Alford, History, II, pp 151-157.

[53] Ibid., p 172.

[54] War Diary, entry for 4 January 44.

[55] Alford, History, II, p 182.

[56] Ibid., p 189.

[57] Ibid., p 190.

[58] Ibid., pp 211-214; 71st Diary, entry for 5 May.

[59] War Department General Order 75, 1944; Alford, History, II, pp 220-223.

[60] Alford, History, II, pp 230-237.

[61] Ibid.

[62] 71st Diary, entry for 10 Jun 44.

[63] Alford, History, II, pp 264-266.

[64] Ibid., pp 288-289.

[65] Argonaut Plan and Annexes, GP-1-SU-RE, 28 Jan-23 Feb 1945, in USAF Collection, USAFHRC; Alford, History, II, p 292.

[66] Alford, History, II, p 306; 71st Diary, entries for 3 and 31 May 1945.

[67] Alford, History, II, p 307; *USAF Credits for the Destruction of Enemy Aircraft, World War II*, USAF Historical Study No 85, AFHRC, 1978, pp 540, 566-567, 580-581.

[68] Alford, History, II, p 310.

CHAPTER FOUR

[1] The 412th and its assigned squadrons were redesignated per GO43, HQ TAC, 26 Jun 46. The 1st Fighter Group was activated and assigned to 12 AF and TAC per GO 9, HQ 12 AF, 3 Jul 46.

[2] Marcelle Size Knaack, Encyclopedia of US Air Force Aircraft and Missile Systems, Vol 1, Post-World War II Fighters, 1945-1973 (Washington: Office of Air Force History, 1978), pp 1-4. Also see the histories of the 1st Fighter Group in file K-GP-1-HI (FTR), 1946-1951 and 1958-1961, The Air Force Historical Research Center (AFHRC), Maxwell AFB, AL. These files are sporadic, and the histories they contain vary greatly in quality and content.

[3] Hist, Tactical Air Command, 1947, Vol I, pp 9-13. Supporting document 19 in this volume is a copy of AAFR 20-15, dated 27 Jun 47; document 38, a letter from Lt Gen Elwood R. Quesada, Commander/TAC, to Maj Gen Glenn O. Barcus, Commander/12 AF, dated 6 Oct 48, discusses the difficulties TAC had in implementing the Wing-Plan. The TAC history cited is available on AFHRC microfilm roll A4022. Also see Thomas A. Sturm, Organization and Responsibility for Air Defense, March 1946 - September 1955, Air Defense Command Historical Study No 9, 1955, pp 58-61 (hereafter cited as Sturm, Air Defense).

[4] GO23, HQ 12 AF, 7 Aug 47.

[5] List, 1st Fighter Wing, April-June 1948, pp 1-2, on AFHRC microfilm roll B0879, frames 296-297.

[6] Ibid., p 2.

[7] Hist, 27th Fighter Squadron, 6-15 May 48, AFHRC file SQ-FI-27-SU.

[8] Hist, 1st Fighter Group Detachment During Operation Combine III, 16 Aug-11 Nov 48, AFHRC file GP-1-SU-OP(FTR).

[9] Hist, 1st Fighter Wing, December 1948-March 1949, AFHRC microfilm roll B0879, frame 0508.

[10] Hist, 1st Fighter Wing and 1st Fighter Group, Jan-Mar 49, microfilm roll B0879, frames 504-695; Lineage, 1st Tactical Fighter Wing, dtd 5 Mar 71; Draft lineage, 1st Tactical Fighter Wing, nd, c. May 82; Condensed Synopsis History of 1st Fighter-Interceptor Wing, nd, c. March 1952, AFHRC file K-WG-1-HI, 47/08/00-52/02/00.

[11] Hist, 1st Fighter Group, Sep 49-Jan 50, AFHRC file K-GP-1-HI(FTR).

[12] Hist, 1st Fighter Wing, Jan 50, AFHRC file K-GP-1-HI (FTR); Hist, 1st Fighter Group, Apr 50, microfilm roll B-0879, frame 1019.

[13] Hist, 1st Fighter (later Fighter-Interceptor) Group, Jan-Jun 50, AFHRC file K-GP-1-HI(FTR); GO14, HQ SAC, 20 Mar 50; Hist, 1st Fighter-Interceptor Wing, Jun 50, microfilm

B0879, frames 1629-1650.

[14] Hist, 1st Fighter-Interceptor Group, Jul-Dec 50, AFHRC file K-GP-1-HI(FTR); Hist, 1st Fighter-Interceptor Wing, Jul-Dec 50, AFHRC microfilm roll M0237, frames 4-411. For the PCS move to Victorville, see GO 7, HQ 1st F-IW, 3 Jul 50 and GO37, HQ 1 F-IW, 14 Jul 50. For the PCS to Griffiss, see OPO 370.5, HQ 4 AF, 30 Jul 50. For the attachment of the group to the EADF, see GO12, HQ 1 F-IW, 15 Aug 50. For the PCS move of the 71st to Pittsburgh, see AAG 370.5, HQ EADF, 18 Oct 50.

[15] Special Hist, 1st Fighter-Interceptor Group, 1st Fighter-Intercepter Wing, WADF, ADC, 4-30 Jun 51, AFHRC file K-GP-1-HI (FTR); Hist, 27th Fighter-Interceptor Squadron, Apr-Jun 51, AFHRC file K-SQ-FI-27-HI.

[16] Sturm, Air Defense, pp 55-59.

[17] Ibid., pp 60-62; GO2, HQ ADC, 11 Jan 52; GO44, HQ ADC, 11 Jan 52.

[18] Lineage, 1st Fighter Group, in Mauer Mauer, ed., Air Force Combat Units of World War II (Maxwell AFB, AL: USAF Historical Division, Air University, 1960), pp 21-24; Lineage, 1st Fighter Group (Air Defense), AFHRC Form 0-34, 22 Apr 77.

[19] Hist, 1st Fighter Group (Air Defense), 1958-1960, AFHRC file K-GP-1-HI; Hist, 1st Fighter Wing (Air Defense), 1958-1960, AFHRC file K-WG-1-HI.

[20] Hist, 1st Fighter Wing (Air Defense), 1 Jan-31 Mar 61, AFHRC file K-WG-1-HI; GO192, HQ ADC, 28 Dec 60.

[21] Hist, 1st Fighter Wing (Air Defense), 1 Jan-31 Mar 61, AFHRC file K-WG-1-HI; Cornett and Johnson, Handbook of Aerospace Defense Organization, pp 69, 107, 111, 132, 135, 151; USAF Lineage and Honors, AFHRC Form 0-34, for the 1st Avionics Maintenance Squadron, dtd 30 Mar 72; 1st CES, 25 Apr 77; 1st CSS, 10 Sep 71; 1st OMS, 30 Mar 72; 1st SPS, 26 Apr 77; 1st Sup Sq, 22 Apr 77; 1st Trans Sq, 25 Apr 77.

[22] Hist, 27th Fighter-Interceptor Squadron, Jul-Dec 61, AFHRC file K-SQ-FI-27-HI.

[23] Hist, 1st Fighter Wing, Dec 62, AFHRC file K-WG-1-HI.

[24] Ibid., 1963.

[25] Ibid., 1964.

[26] Ibid., 1965-1969.

[27] Ibid., 1965-1966.

[28] Ibid., Jan-Mar 67; Hist, 71st Fighter-Interceptor Squadron, Apr-Jun 67, AFHRC file K-SQ-FI-71-HI; Hist, 27th Fighter-Interceptor Squadron, Jan-Dec 67, AFHRC file K-SQ-FI-

27-HI.

[29] Special Study, History of the Detroit Contingency, 24 Jul-4 Aug 67, AFHRC file K-WG-1-HI.

[30] Hist, 71st Fighter-Interceptor Squadron, Jul-Sep 68, AFHRC file K-SQ-FI-71-HI; Hist, 1st FW(AD), Oct-Dec 69, AFHRC file K-WG-1-HI.

[31] Hist, 1st Fighter Wing (Air Defense), Oct-Dec 69, AFHRC file K-WG-1-HI.

Notes, pages 73-76

CHAPTER FIVE

[1] For information on Gen Momyer's unit designation directive, see Staff Summary Sheet, HQ TAC DCS/Plans Organization and Resources Division to TAC Commander, subj: Illustrious Designators for TAC Airlift Forces, 9 Apr 71, Supporting Document 86 in the July 1970 - June 1971 History of TAC, Vol II. As of that date, the plans staff reported that "all of TAC's fighter and reconnaissance forces will soon be tied with units having outstanding histories." The redesignation of the four-digit units began on 15 October 1969, with the redesignation of several. See, for example, HQ TAC SO G-167, 27 Aug 69, which inactivated the 4525th Fighter Weapons Wing and the 4536th, 4537th, 4538th, and 4539th Fighter Weapons Squadrons at Nellis AFB, Nevada, and activated the 57th FWW and the 65, 66, 414, and 422 FWS in their place.

[2] HQ ADC Movement Order 3, 3 Aug 70.

[3] HQ TAC SO G-150, 2 Sep 70.

[4] MacDill Herald, 2 Oct 70, in History, 1 TFW, Oct-Dec 70, Supporting Document 3.

[5] Ibid.

[6] History, 1 TFW, Oct-Dec 70, p 5.

[7] TAC Regulation 23-67, Tactical Fighter Wings, 17 Jun 69. The extended quote is from para 1a; the shorter quote is from para 1b.

[8] TAC Regulation 23-39, Training Wings/Groups, 28 Feb 72, para 1.

[9] TAC Regulation 23-65, Training Squadrons, 9 Mar 70, para 1.

[10] HQ TAC SO G-128, 24 May 71; HQ TAC SO G-130, 24 May 1971.

[11] HQ TAC SO G-230, 9 Sep 71; HQ TAC SO GA-112, 5 Apr 72.

[12] Marcelle Size Knaack, Encyclopedia of US Air Force Aircraft and Missile Systems, Volume I, Post World War II Fighters, 1945 - 1973 (Washington: Office of Air Force History,) 1978), p 334; letter, Gen Momyer to Gen Ryan, subj: F-15/A-X Beddown Proposal, 11 May 1972.

[13] Staff Summary Sheet, HQ TAC DCS/Plans to TAC Commander, subj: Langley Wing Designator, 30 Mar 74; letter, HQ TAC DCS/Plans to HQ USAF Director of Manpower and Organization, subj: Request for Programming Change, 4 Apr 74. According to the 30 Mar 74 staff summary sheet, the 1970 study ranked the units by awarding points for "total months in combat, total hours, total months on active duty, and consideration of specific acts, zones of operations and overall unit history." Based on these criteria, the 1st TFW likely outscored the other units by a wide margin.

[14] Message, CSAF/PRPO to CINCPACAF/XOX, subj: DAF Movement Directive (56 Special Operations Wing), 141401Z May 75.

[15] HQ TAC SO GA-12, 10 Jun 75.

[16] Capts Tom Lennon and Jim Wray, Bringing the F-15 to Operational Readiness (Langley AFB, VA: 1st TFW, 1977). This brief monograph, prepared by personnel closely involved in the wing's progress toward operationally ready status, discusses the wing's first eighteen months with the F-15 in great detail. 4SO GB-116, HQ USAF, 1 Mar 78.

[17] Ibid., pp 49-52.

[18] HQ TAC SO GA-15, 5 Apr 76; HQ TAC SO GA-28, 29 Mar 77.

[19] Lennon and Wray, F-15 Readiness, p 7.

[20] Ibid., pp 6-7. The quote is from p 7.

[21] HQ TAC SO GA-31, 8 Apr 77.

[22] 1 TFW histories, prepared quarterly, contain chronologies that list the deployments.

[23] "Langley F-15 Jets Flunk Readiness Test," Hampton VA Daily Press, 12 Jun 80, p 1. Also see "Half of F-15s Stay on Ground," Hampton VA Times Herald, 12 Jun 80, p 1; "Fighter Wing Fails Review," Norfolk VA Virginian-Pilot, 13 Jun 80, p 1; "Nuts and Bolts Shortages Idle Half of F-15s," Hampton VA Daily Press, 14 Jun 80, p 1.

[24] General Fischer's comments were noted by the author at the 19 August 1982 press conference.

[25] Information on this deployment can be found in the 1 TFW history covering the period April - September 1983.

[26] HQ USAF SO GB-004, 11 Jan 85.

Index **155**

INDEX

A

Aberdeen Proving Ground, Maryland, 28
Adamson, H. J., representative of Assistant Secretary of War for
  Air on "Arctic Patrol Flight," 27
Advanced Pursuit Training School, 19 - 20
Aerial Gunnery Camp, 21
Aerospace Defense Command, see also Air Defense Command
  1st Fighter Wing transferred from, 73
Agan, Colonel Arthur C., commander, 1st Fighter Group, taken POW, 53
Air Base Headquarters and Third Air Base Squadron (formerly Station
  Complement, Selfridge Field), 32
Air Corps Demonstration, Declaration of Independence
  Sesquicentennial Exhibition, 23
Air Corps/Anti-Aircraft Service exercise, 28
Air Defense Command, see also Aerospace Defense Command
  1st Fighter-Interceptor Wing assigned to, 63 - 65
  reestablished as major command, 63
  under control of Continental Air Command, 61
Air Force Bands
  589th Air Force Band, 74
Air Force Outstanding Unit Awards
  presented to 1st Tactical Fighter Wing 77, 80
air mail duty, 30 - 31
air shows for municipal airfields, 26
aircraft
  A-12, 31
  Albatros D.V, 5, 7
  B-6A, 30, 31
  B-12A, 31
  B-17, 45 - 47
  B-24, 47, 52
  B-26, 25, 50 - 51
  B-57, 74 - 75
  C-1, 22 - 23, 25, 27
  C-9, 27, 28
  C-27A, 31
  C-47, 45
  C-130, 66
  Curtiss Hawk, 29 (see also P-6, P-6A, and P-6E)
  EC-135, 78
  F-4, 74 - 75
  F-15, 76 - 80 (also see TF-15, YF-15)
  F-80, 59, 61
  F-86, 59, 65

assigned to 94th Fighter Squadron, 61 - 62
  maintenance and modifications, 61 - 62
F-104 Delta Dagger interceptor, 65
F-106 Delta Dart, 65 - 66
F-106A, 66
F-106B, 66
Fiesler Storch, 50
Fokker, 8, 12 - 13
FW-190, 47, 48, 50, 53
FW-200 Condor, 46
Ju-52, 50
Ju-88, 49
ME-109, 47 - 48, 50
ME-110, 48
Nieuport 28, 2 - 7, 9
O-2K, 27
O-39, 31
O-43A, 31
P-1, 22 - 23, 25 - 29
  used in "Arctic Patrol Flight," 27
  used in joint Army-Navy exercises, 28
P-1A, 22 - 23
P-1B, 23 - 24
P-6, 29
P-6A, 30
P-6E, 29 - 30
P-12, 28 - 29
P-12B, 28
P-12C, 29 - 30
P-12D, 29 - 30
P-12E, 29 - 31
P-16, 29 - 30
P-26, 33, 35
  engine and armament, 34 - 35
P-26A, 31 - 33
P-26C, 33, 35
P-35, 33
P-36, 33 - 34
P-38, 25, 35, 43, 45 - 53
  description, 34 - 35
P-38F, 45
P-38J, 52
P-40, 46
P-43, 43
P-80 Shooting Star, 59, 61
Thomas-Morse MB-3, 20
T-33 trainer, 66

Index

TF-15, 70 (also see F-15, YF-15)
XP-6C, 30
YF-15, 76 (also see F-15, TF-15)
YP-12K, 31
Y1P-16, 30 - 31
Y1P-36, 33
aircraft maintenance units (AMUs), 79
Army Air Force Regulation 20-15, 59
Aisne-Marne campaign, 9 - 10, 21 (see also Chateau Thierry campaign)
Allen, Brigadier General Jesse M., DCS Plans, TAC, 76
Allison V-1710 engine, P-38 equipped with, 35
Anderson, Capt. Wyman D., 62
Andrews, Lieutenant Colonel (later Major General) Frank M.
   assumed command of 1st Pursuit Group, 30
   commmander, GHQ Air Force (as Major General), 32
   relinquished command of 1st Pursuit Group to Major Royce, 31
Arctic Patrol Flight, 27
Arnold, General Henry H., Chief, Army Air Forces, 43 - 44
Atkinson, Major Bert M., 1 - 2, 5
   commander of 1st Pursuit Group, 6 - 8
   assumes command of 1st Pursuit Wing, 10
Atlantic Command, 78
Aversa, Italy, mission over, 51
Aviation Mobilization Camp No. 2, 2
Aviation Training Center, Issoudun, France, 2
Avon Park Gunnery Range, Florida, 73, 75, 77

B

Balbo, General Italo, 30
Bangor Air Defense Sector, 26th Air Division, 65
bases (US)
   Barksdale Field LA, 32 - 33
   Bergstrom AFB TX, 61
   Bolling Field DC, 24 - 25
   Bowman Field KY, 30, 32
   Chanute Field IL, 28, 32
   Dow Field ME, 45
   Eglin AFB FL, 61 - 62
   Ellington Field TX, 20
   Elmendorf AFB AK, 65
   George AFB CA, 62 - 64
   Griffiss AFB NY, 63
   Hamilton AFB CA, 73
      1st Fighter Wing transferred to, 66
   Kelly Field TX, 19 - 20, 23 - 25
      1st Pursuit Group moved from Selfridge Field to, 19

27th Aero Squadron organized at, 5
94th and 95th Aero Squadrons organized at, 1
147th Aero Squadron organized at, 5
185th Night Pursuit Squadron organized at, 12
Langley AFB VA, 76 - 78
  1st Tactical Fighter Wing based at, 77 - 78
  repavement of main runway, 80
Langley Field VA, 32
  20th Bombardment Squadron located at, 30
  36th Pursuit Squadron transferred to, 28 - 29
  air demonstrations at, 22, 25
  General Headquarters Air Force (GHQAF) established at, 32
Luke AFB AZ, 76 - 77
MacDill AFB FL, 73 - 75
  1st Tactical Fighter Wing assigned to, 73 - 74
  1st Tactical Fighter Wing transferred to Langley from, 76 - 77
  56th Tactical Fighter Wing assigned to, 76 - 77
Malmstrom AFB MT, 66
March Field CA, 35, 43
  1st Fighter Wing activated at, 60
  95th Bombardment Squadron located at, 25
  412th Fighter Group located at, 59
Mather Field CA, 28
Maxwell Field AL, 26
McChord AFB WA, 79
Nellis AFB NV, 78 - 79
Norton AFB CA, 64
Oscoda MI, 22, 29 - 31
  Aerial Gunnery Camp at, 21
  cold weather equipment tests, 33
  Colonel Lindbergh visited, 25
  field exercises at, 32
  winter maneuvers at, 22
Patrick AFB, Florida, 65
Patterson Field, Ohio, 29 - 30
Phelps Collins Air National Guard Base, Alpena, Michigan, 80
Pope Field, North Carolina, 24
Selfridge AFB, Michigan, 64 - 66
Selfridge Field, Michigan, 19 - 30, 32 - 34, 43
  1st Pursuit Group left for Kelly Field from, 19
  1st Pursuit Group organized at, 13, 19
  1st Pursuit Group returned to, 20
  36th Pursuit Squadron activated at, 28
  location of Mitchell Trophy race, 33
  Provisional Cold Weather Test Group formed at, 29, 31, 33
Tyndall AFB FL, 65
Victorville (later George) AFB CA, 62

Index

Volk Field WI, 65
Wright Field OH, 22
Wurtsmith AFB MI, 66
Battle of Midway, 45
Beckham, Captain Dwight S., one of the "Sabre Dancers," 62
Biskra, Algeria, 1st Fighter Group at, 49
Bitburg Air Base, Germany, 78
Bittner, Lieutenant Clement L., one of the "Sabre Dancers," 62
Bluie West Eight (BW 8) Field, Greenland, 46
Bluie West One (BW 1) Army Air Field, Greenland, 46
Bonnell, Major Geoffrey, commander, 147th Aero Squadron, 7
Brett, Major George H., commander, 1st Pursuit Group, 30
brigades (Army)
   1st Air Brigade, 8
   2d Brigade, 66
   3d Brigade, 66
Britt, Lieutenant Colonel John, 27th Tactical Fighter Squadron, 77
Brooks, Captain Arthur E., commander, 1st Pursuit Group, 19
Buckley, Lieutenant Harold, 8

C

Campbell, First Lieutenant Douglas, 2, 4
   first U. S. World War I ace, 7
Caserta, Italy, 1st Fighter Group at, 53
Cazaux, France, gunnery training school at, 3, 5
centers
   1st Pursuit Organization and Training Center, 1 - 5
     established at Villeneuve-les-Vertus, 1
     moved to Epiez, 3
     transferred from Epiez to Gencoult, 3
Chambers, Lieutenant Reed, 4 - 5
Champagne-Marne campaign, 21
Chateau d'un du Rhumel, 1st Fighter Group based at, 49
Chateau Thierry campaign, 9 - 10 (see also Aisne-Marne campaign)
Churchill, Winston, 53
Civilian Conservation Corps, 29
Coligny airfield, 3
Company K, 3d Provisional Aero Squadron, 5
   see also 27th Aero Squadron, 5
Continental Air Command
   1st Fighter-Interceptor Wing assigned to, 62
   assumed jurisdiction over TAC and ADC, 61
   established 1 December 1948, 61
Congressional Medal of Honor, 12
Craft, Lieutenant Colonel Larry
   commander, 27th Tactical Fighter Squadron, 77

Creighton, Captain Richard D., 62
Crumley, Lieutenant Newton, 31
Cuban Missile Crisis, 65
Culbert, Lieutenant Kenneth P., 6
Curtiss V-157A engine, 29
Curtiss V-1570C engine, 29

D

Daily Press, Hampton, Virginia, 79
Danielson, Lieutenant Warren
   made last aerial kill for 1st Fighter Group in WWII, 53
Davis, Major Michael, commander of 27th Aero Squadron, 5
Day Bombardment Group, 10
Detroit Air Defense Sector, 65
Distinguished Unit Citations, won by 1st Fighter Group, 50 - 52
Dittaino, Sicily, 1st Fighter Group at airfield, 51
divisions (Air Force and Army)
   2d Armored Division (Army), 61
   23d Air Division, 66
   26th Air Division, 66
   27th Air Division, 63
   28th Air Division, 66
   30th Air Division, 65 - 66
   34th Air Division, 65
   36th Air Division, 66
   82d Airborne Division (Army), 66
   101st Airborne Division (Army), 66
   836th Air Division
      1st Tactical Fighter Wing assigned to, 74
      inactivated, 75
Doubleday, Lieutenant Daniel C., 32
Duluth International Airport, Minnesota, 66

E

E-3 Airborne Warning and Control System, 79
Eastern Air Defense Force (EADF), Continental Air Command, 63
Eighth Air Force, 46
Eiland, Captain John D.
   scored first combat kill for the 27th Fighter Squadron, 48
Elmendorf, Captain Hugh M., commander, 94th Pursuit Squadron, 24
Epiez, 4 - 6
   1st Pursuit Organization and Training Center located at, 3 - 4
Exercise College Cadence, 66

Index

F

Farley, Lieutenant Robert E., 62
Fechet, Brigadier General James E.
   Air Service Chief of Staff, 23, 25
Fifteenth Air Force
   1st Fighter Wing transferred to, 61
   1st Fighter-Interceptor Wing assigned to, 62
   organized in 1943, 51 - 52
First Air Force, 65 - 66
First Army, 11
Fischer, Brigadier General Eugene H.
   commander, 1st Tactical Fighter Wing, 80
Flynn, Captain Walter F., 52
Foggia airfield, Italy, mission over, 50, 52
Foulois, Brigadier (later Major) General Benjamin D.
   Chief of the Air Corps, 30
   Chief of the Air Service, American Expeditionary Forces, 1
Fourth Air Force, 61 - 62
French VIII Army, 4

G

Gambut, Libya, 1st Fighter Group moved to, 51
Garman, Captain Ralph, 35
   assumed command of 1st Fighter Group, 48
Gencoult airfield, France, 4 - 6, 8
   94th Aero Squadron moved from Epiez to, 3 - 4
   95th Aero Squadron moved to, 5 - 6
General Headquarters Air Force (GHQAF), 32
George Washington Bicentennial Military Tournament, 29
Gioia del Colle, Italy, 1st Fighter Group based at, 51
Gnome rotary engine, used in Nieuport, 9
Goering, Hermann, 8
Grant, Lieutenant Alfred A., commander, 27th Aero Squadron, 10
Great Depression, 29
groups
   1st Corps Observation Group, 6, 8
      AEF's first flying group, 6
   1st Fighter Group, 45 - 53, 59 - 62
      activated 3 July 1946, 59
      deactivated on 16 October 1945, 53
      headquarters assigned to 1st Fighter Wing, 60
      new designation of 1st Pursuit Group (15 May 1942), 45
      number of sorties, kills, and losses in WWII, 53
   1st Fighter Group (Air Defense)
      redesignated 20 June 1955, 64

headquarters inactivated, 65
1st Fighter-Interceptor Group, 62 - 64
   assigned to 1st Fighter-Interceptor Wing, 62
   headquarters moved from Griffiss AFB to George AFB, 63
   headquarters stationed at Griffiss AFB, 63
   inactivated on 6 Feb 1952, 64
1st Pursuit Group, 1, 6 - 13, 19 - 35, 75
   65th anniversary, 5 May 1983, 80
   activated 22 August 1919, 19
   assigned to 2d Wing, GHQAF, 32
   disbanded, 13
   emblem, 21
   participation at 1933 World's Fair, 30
   organized 5 May 1918, 6
   number of kills in WWI, 12 - 13
   redesignated 1st Pursuit Group (Interceptor), 34
1st Pursuit Group (Interceptor), 34, 43 - 45
   new designation, 6 December 1939, 34
   personnel strength in 1942, 43
   redesignated 1st Fighter Group, 45
2d Bombardment Group, 19
   provided aircraft for 1926 maneuvers, 22
   provided aircraft for 1936 maneuvers, 32
2d Pursuit Group, 9, 11
3d Attack Group, 19
   94th Pursuit Squadron attached to, 30
   provided aircraft for 1926 maneuvers, 22
   provided aircraft for Provisional Cold Weather Test Group, 31
   provided aircraft for 1936 maneuvers, 32
3rd Pursuit Group, 9, 11
5th Air Depot Group, 45
5th Pursuit Group, Third Army, 13
7th Bombardment Group, 25, 31
8th Pursuit Group, 28, 33
   36th Pursuit Squadron transferred to, 29
12th Groupe de Combat, 1
12th Observation Group, 31
14th Fighter Group, 48, 50
20th Pursuit Group, 28
31st Fighter Group, 45
51st Pursuit Group, 43
60th Transport Group, 45
67th Reconnaissance Group, 60
80th Pursuit Group, 43
82d Pursuit Group, 43, 48
82d Fighter Group, 50, 52 - 53
97th Bombardment Group, 45

Index

319th Bombardment Group, 51
320th Bombardment Group, 51
412th Fighter Group, 59
506th Aircraft Control & Warning Group, 60
4708th Air Base Group, 66
Ginn, Lieutenant Malcolm
   suggested design for 27th Aero Squadron insignia, 7

H

Hall, Captain James N., 5
Harmon, Captain James, commander, 94th Fighter Squadron, 47
Hartney, Major Harold E., 10 - 12
   commander, 27th Aero Squadron, 5, 7, 9
   took command of 1st Pursuit Group, 10
Hat-in-the-Ring emblem, 10, 47
   adopted by 94th Aero Squadron, 3
   adopted by Rickenbacker for automobile company logo, 21
   reassigned to the 94th Fighter Squadron, 44
Hatch, Lieutenant Herbert B., 52
Headquarters and HQ Squadron, 1st Pursuit Group
   formerly 1st Pursuit HQ and 56th and 57th Service Squadrons, 32
Hispano-Suiza engine, 9
Huffer, Major John F., commander, 94th Aero Squadron, 2 - 3

I

Ilfrey, Lieutenant Jack, 47 - 48
Israel, Major Robert S., Jr.
   commander, 1st Pursuit Group, 43
   promoted to Lieutenant Colonel, 43
   reassigned to 82d Pursuit Group, 43
Issoudun, Aviation Training Center, 1 - 2, 5
Italian Trans-Atlantic Flight, 30

J

Jagdeschwader 1, 8 (see also Richtofen Flying Circus)
Jeffers, Lieutenant John, 10
Jet Pilot, 62
Johnson, Major Davenport, commander, 95th Aero Squadron, 3

K

Kirby, Major Maxwell
   made last aerial kill of WWI, 13
Korean War, 64

L

Lafayette Escadrille, 21
Lanphier, Major Thomas G., commander, 1st Pursuit Group, 22, 25
LeMay, Lieutenant Curtis E., 30 - 31
Lentz, Lieutenant J. C. Harrison, 49
Lindbergh, Colonel Charles A., 25
Low, Lieutenant Seth
   commander, 185th Night Pursuit Squadron, 12
   took command of 95th Aero Squadron, 3
Lowry, Lieutenant Durwood O.
   first Air Corps pilot to die in air mail operation, 31
Lucera, Italy, 53
Lufbery, Major Raoul, 2
   killed in action, 6
   number of kills, 6, 13
Luke, Lieutenant Frank, 10, 12
   number of kills, 13

M

Maison Blanche, 71st and 94th Fighter Squadrons at, 48
Maloney, Lieutenant Thomas E., 53
Marne front, 8
Marr, Major Kenneth, commander, 94th Aero Squadron, 10
Martin, Lieutenant Colonel Donald W.
   commander, 47th (then 94th) Tactical Fighter Squadron, 75
Mateur, North Africa, 1st Fighter Group stationed near, 51
McDonnell-Douglas Aircraft Company, 75
McIntosh, Lieutenant Frank J.
   led mission over Aversa, 51
McNeil, Colonel Travis R.
   commander, 1st Tactical Fighter Wing, 74
Mediterranean Air Command, 49
Meuse-Argonne offensive, 10 - 12, 21
Miller, Captain James E., commander, 95th Aero Squadron,
Miller, Lieutenant Colonel George H.
   commander, 1st Tactical Fighter Wing, 77
Minty, Lieutenant Russell J., 22
Mitchell Trophy Race, 20 - 21, 33
Mitchell, Colonel William
   Air Commander, Zone of Advance, 1
   commanded 1st Air Brigade, 8
   donated John L. Mitchell Trophy, 20
Momyer, General William W.
   Commander, Tactical Air Command, 73, 75
Monserrato, Sardinia, airfield, 51

Index

Morey, First Lieutenant John D.
   commander, 147th Aero Squadron, 5

N

Nakhon Phanom Airport, Thailand, 76
Natcher, First Lieutenant Fred
   commander, 95th Aero Squadron, 1
National Air Races, 20
Ninth Air Force, 75 - 76
North African campaign, 47 - 50
North African Strategic Air Force, 50
North American Aviation Company, 62
Nouvion, Algeria
   1st Fighter Group HQ and 27th Fighter Squadron based at, 47 - 48

O

Operation Argonaut, 53
Operation Bolero, movement of AAF units to England, 44 - 46, 48 - 49
Operation Dragoon, invasion of Southern France, 53
Operation Prized Eagle, 79
Operation Ready Eagle, 78
Operation Red Flag VI, 78
Osan Air Base, Korea, 66

P

Pacific Air Forces (PACAF), 76
Patrick, Major General Mason M., Chief of the Air Service, 22
Peterson, Captain David, 4
Ploesti Romano-Americano Oil Refinery, bombing of, 52
Pratt & Whitney radial engine, 29
Pratt and Whitney R-1340-27 Wasp engine, 31
Pritchard, Captain Frank H., 24
Production Oriented Maintenance Organization (POMO), 79
Project Peace Reef, 75

R

Rankin, Captain John G., 1
Rembercourt, 1st Pursuit Group based at, 10, 13
Richardson, Captain William N.
   diarist of 71st Fighter Squadron, 53
Richthofen, Baron Manfred von, 5
Richtofen Flying Circus, 8 (see also Jagdeschwader 1)
Rickenbacker, Edward V., 2, 4 - 5

    adopted Hat-in-the-Ring emblem for automobile company logo, 21
    morale-boosting tour, 43 - 44
    number of kills in WWI, 13
    on problems in Army Air Forces, 43 - 44
    took command of 94th Aero Squadron, 10
    visited First Fighter Group, 47
Roberts, Captain Newell O., 48
Roosevelt, Captain Philip J., 1
Roosevelt, President Franklin D., 53
    ordered Air Corps to carry mail, 30
Royce, Major Ralph
    commander, 1st Pursuit Group, 27 - 28, 31
    flew first P-36 to Selfridge field, 33
Rush, Major George A., operations officer, 1st Fighter Group, 50
Ryan, General John D., Air Force Chief of Staff, 76

S

"Sabre Dancers," aerial demonstration team, 62
St Mihiel campaign, 10, 21
Saints, 1st Pursuit Group based at, 9
Salsola airfield, Italy, 51, 53
Schafer, Lieutenant Joseph D., 46
Shahan, Lieutenant Elza D., 46
    received Silver Star, 49
Sherry, Major Alden B.
    intelligence officer, 1st Fighter Group, 47
Smith, Captain John D., 62
Smith, First Lieutenant J. Bayard H.
    first commander of the 94th Aero Squadron, 1
Southeast Asia, 65
Spaatz, Major Carl, commander, 1st Pursuit Group, 20
squadrons
    6th Airborne Command and Control Squadron, 78
    17th Aero Squadron, 20
    17th Pursuit Squadron, 29
        based at Bowman Field, Kentucky, 30
        conversion to Boeing P-26As, 31
        deactivation, 34
        enlisted personnel cuts, 32
        "Great Snow Owl" emblem, 21
        training at Barksdale, 32
    27th Aero Squadron
        organization and early history, 5
        joins 1st Pursuit Group, 6
        designs insignia, 7
        scores first combat kill, 7

Index

    Lieutenant Frank Luke, member of, 12
    demobilized, 13
    assembled at Selfridge Field, Michigan, 19
    emblem approved, 21
27th Fighter Squadron
    stationed in Iceland, 46
    scores first kill in ETO in WWII, 46
    moves to the United Kingdom, 46
    moves from Great Britain to Gibraltar, 47
    combat kills in WWII, 53
    "Sabre Dancers," 62
27th Fighter-Interceptor Squadron
    assigned to Griffiss AFB, New York, 63
    attached to 103d Fighter-Interceptor Wing, 63
    assigned to 4711th Air Defense Wing, 64
    moved to Bangor, Maine, 65
27th Pursuit Squadron
    Lieutenant Curtis E. LeMay, member of, 30
    deploys aircraft to Chanute Field, Illinois, for maneuvers, 32
    participates in cold weather test, 33
    receives first P-38 Lightnings, 34
27th Tactical Fighter Squadron
    assigned to 1st Tactical Fighter Wing, 75
    transferred to Langley AFB, Virginia, 76
    receives first F-15, 77
    deploys first F-15s to Red Flag, 78
71st Fighter-Interceptor Squadron
    moved to Griffiss AFB, New York, 63
    attached to 103d Fighter-Interceptor Wing, 63
    assigned to 4708th Air Defense Wing, 64
    assigned to 1st Fighter Wing, Air Defense, 64
    wins F-106 division of William Tell, 1965, 65
    assigned to 328th Fighter Wing, Air Defense, 66
71st Pursuit Squadron
    activated, 34
    emblem, 43
    stationed at Goxhill, Scotland, 46
    first WWII combat casualty, 47
    moved to North Africa, 47 - 48
    WWII combat kills, 53
71st Tactical Fighter Squadron
    assigned to 1st Tactical Fighter Wing, 75
    achieves operationally-ready status in F-15, 77
94th Aero Squadron, 1 - 7, 9 - 11, 19 - 20
    assigned to 5th Pursuit Group, 13
    demobilized, 13
    dispatched to Selfridge Field, 19

    number of kills and losses in WWI, 7, 13
  94th Fighter Squadron, 46 - 50, 52 - 53, 59 - 62
    assigned to 1st Fighter Wing, 60
    F-86s assigned to, 61
    number of kills in WWII, 53
    Operation Bolero, 46
    redesignated 94th Fighter-Interceptor Squadron, 62
  94th Fighter-Interceptor Squadron, 63 - 65
    assigned to 1st Fighter Group (Air Defense), 64
    assigned to 4705th Air Defense Wing, WADF, 64
  94th Pursuit Squadron, 24, 28 - 35
    air mail duty, 31
    based at Patterson Field, Ohio, 30
    emblem, 21, 43 - 44
    enlisted personnel cuts, 32
    maneuvers, 34
    participated in joint Army/Navy exercises, 28
    Rickenbacker visited, 44
  95th Aero Squadron, 1 - 3, 5 - 9, 19 - 20
    assigned to 1st Pursuit Group, 6, 19
    demobilized, 13
    number of kills and losses in WWI, 13
    reported to 1st Pursuit Organization and Training Center, 1
  95th Bombardment Squadron, 25
  95th Pursuit Squadron
    "Kicking Mule" emblem, 21
    inactivated, 25
  103rd Aero Squadron, 21
  147th Aero Squadron, 5 - 7, 9, 19 - 20
    assigned to 1st Pursuit Group, 6
    demobilized, 13
    number of kills and losses in WWI, 13
    organized, 5
    redesignated 17th Aero Squadron, 20
    reported to 1st Pursuit Organization and Training Center, 5
  185th Night Pursuit Squadron, 12
  188th Fighter-Interceptor Squadron, 63
  325th Observation Squadron, Organized Reserve, 30
  608th Aircraft Control & Warning Squadron, 60
Stace, Lieutenant Donald F.
  won the first Mitchell trophy race, 20
Sterling, Lieutenant John M.
  won Mitchell trophy, 33
Stone, Colonel John N.
  commander, 1st Fighter Group, 46
Strategic Air Command
  1st Fighter Wing transferred to, 61

Index

1st Fighter-Interceptor Wing assigned to, 62

T

Tactical Air Command
  1st Fighter Group assigned to, 59
  1st Fighter Wing assigned to, 60
  under control of Continental Air Command, 61
Tafaroui, North Africa, airfield at, 47
Taliaferro, Lieutenant Russell E.
  one of the "Sabre Dancers," 62
Taylor, Lieutenant Mervin M.
  one of the "Sabre Dancers," 62
Tedder, Air Marshall Sir Arthur, 49
Tonquin, 1st Pursuit Group based at, 7, 9
Toul, France, 7, 12
Truman, President Harry S., 62
Tunis, North Africa, capture of, 50
Twelfth Air Force, 48, 51
  1st Fighter Group assigned to, 59
  1st Fighter Wing assigned to, 60
  assigned to Continental Air Command, 61
27th Squadron, see Squadrons, 27th
Twin Wasp engine, 33

V

Verdun campaign, 10, 21
Vietnam, 65
VIIIth Fighter Command, 46
Villeneuve-les-Vertus, France, 1 - 5
  1st Pursuit Organization and Training Center established at, 1
  Training Center moved to Epiez from, 3, 5 - 6

W

Walters, Lieutenant Paul
  medical officer, 94th Aero Squadron, 3
Wehner, Lieutenant Joseph, 12
Wentworth, Lieutenant Paul
  sketched Hat-in-the-Ring emblem, 3
Western Air Defense Force, Continental Air Command, 63
wing-base plan, 59 - 60, 64
wings
  1st Fighter Wing
    1st Fighter Group attached to, 59
    activated on 15 August 1947, 60

    attached to 22d Bomb Wing, 61
    mission, 60 - 61
    organization of, 60
    redesignated 1st Fighter-Interceptor Wing, 62
    transferred to Fourth Air Force, 61
    transferred to SAC and Fifteenth Air Force, 61
  1st Fighter Wing (Air Defense)
    activated 18 October 1956, 64
    assigned to 34th Air Division, First Air Force, 65
  1st Fighter-Interceptor Wing
    assigned to Air Defense Command, 63
    assigned to Fifteenth Air Force and SAC, 62
    assigned to Fourth Air Force and ConAC, 62
    inactivated on 6 February 1952, 64
    organization of, 62 - 63
    personnel reductions, 64
    redesignation of 1st Fighter Wing, 62
  1st Pursuit Wing, 10 - 11
  2d Wing, GHQAF, 32
    1st Pursuit Group assigned to, 32
  3d Wing, GHQAF, 32
  22d Bombardment Wing, 61 - 62
  103d Fighter-Interceptor Wing, 63
  4705th Air Defense Wing, WADF, 64
  4708th Air Defense Wing, EADF, 64
  4711th Air Defense Wing, EADF, 64
Wings, 23
Winslow, Lieutenant Alan, 4 - 5
World War I, 1 - 13
  Aisne-Marne campaign, 9 - 10, 21 (also Chateau Thierry campaign)
  Champagne-Marne campaign, 21
  Marne front, 7 - 8
  Meuse-Argonne offensive, 10 - 12, 21
  number of kills and losses, 7, 12 - 13
  St Mihiel campaign, 10, 21
  Verdun campaign, 10, 21
World War II, 43 - 53
  Battle of Midway, 45
  bombing of Ploesti Romano-Americano Oil Refinery, 52 - 53
  capture of Tunis, North Africa, 50
  mission over Aversa, Italy, 51
  mission over Foggia airfield, Italy, 50
  North African campaign, 47 - 50
  number of kills and losses, 53
  Operation Argonaut, 53
  Operation Bolero
    movement of AAF units to England, 44 - 46, 48 - 49

Index

    Operation Dragoon, invasion of Southern France, 53
    Yalta Conference, 53
World's Fair (1933), 30

Y

Yalta Conference, 53
Youks-les-Bains, 94th Fighter Squadron based at, 48
Young, Lieutenant William H.
    first WWII casualty of 1st Fighter Group, 47